IT HAPPENED AGAIN

It Happened Again

HELEN BOWEN GRAY

RINNAH
PRESS

This book was typeset by
ASHFIELD PRESS PUBLISHING SERVICES
for

© Helen Bowen Gray, 2005, Rinnah Press

Unless otherwise indicated, Scripture quotations are from the New
International Version (NIV) © 1973.1978,1983 by the International Bible
Society. Used by permission.

Scripture quotations marked (KJV) are taken from the King James Version
of the Bible.

ISBN: 0-9551002-0-8

All rights reserved. No part of this publication may be reproduced, stored
in a retrieval system or transmitted in any form or by any means,
electronic, mechanical, photocopying, recording or otherwise,
without the prior, written permission of the publisher.

This book is sold subject to the condition that it shall not, by way of trade
or otherwise, be lent, resold, hired out, or otherwise circulated without
the publisher's prior consent in any form of binding or cover other
than that in which it is published and without a similar condition
including this condition being imposed on the subsequent purchaser.

Designed by Susan Waine, Ashfield Press
Printed in Ireland by ßetaprint Limited, Dublin

Contents

Foreword	7
Acknowledgements	8
Preface	9
Encounter with God	11
To love and to cherish till death us do part (Part One)	23
To love and to cherish till death us do part (Part Two)	47
Single Parent	76
Heaven	97
Redirected Love	104
He will give His angels charge over you	113
Tidings of comfort and joy	119
Promise of provision	125
I dare to dream	130
Emotional Healing	140
A dream comes true	205
Notes	217

IN LOVING MEMORY

I cherish the memory of my parents Isaac Lloyd and Georgina Margaret Rountree whom I have come to understand better since writing my story.

DEDICATION

I dedicate this book to my daughters, Esther Joy and Eleanor and thank them for their unswerving support through out this project. I couldn't have done this without them. I hope this account relating to their fathers will fill in some of the blank pages in their past.

Foreword

I have listened to Helen's story since she became a parishioner some seven years ago. It has gradually unfolded. Her book, "It Happened Again" adds another dimension to her remarkable life. It is a story of pain, hope and Christian victory in the experience of parturition.

Helen writes authoritatively as a woman and as a Christian, tracing the events of her journey with Christ, who at times, must have seemed remote in the isolation following the deaths of her two young husbands.

Her book is compelling reading. It is a resource to keep next to your Bible. Read it again and again. Like so many accounts of great missionaries of the Christian faith, this book will inspire, comfort and lead to a greater understanding of God's purpose in Christ.

Paul's words resonate in Helen's pain bringing a hope, now shared,

"For I am convinced that neither death nor life...nor anything else...will be able to separate us from the love of God that is in Christ Jesus our Lord." (Rom 8:38) I hope that we too will find ressurrection assurance as we explore these pages.

CANON TREVOR SULLIVAN, *Rector.*
Ardrahan, Easter Sunday 2005

ACKNOWLEDGEMENTS

I wish to thank those who have helped and advised me in the preparation of this project: Roberta Collins, Trevor Sullivan, Kate McMahon and Patricia Stevens. They gave their time in reading the manuscript and offering invaluable suggestions.

I want to express my gratitude to all those who have given me support with regular phone calls and prayers including Dorothy Clarke, Ellen Sullivan, Fiona Burke, Mary O Neill and Eileen Quinn.

Most of all I am so grateful to John for his love and patience shown in so many different ways, especially in acting as a soundboard to test my ideas.

Preface

The reason I wrote my story is that when I told the events of my life to several people some years ago, they responded enthusiastically with remarks like, "It's sounds like something you'd read in a novel. Did you ever think of writing a book?" I replied that the thought had come to me shortly after the second tragedy, "One day you will write your story and share with others how you overcame your difficulties. "In the following pages I share my story with you, how my life was shattered, not once but twice, through tragic events. Each time it seemed I had lost everything, but I want to show how I gained the will to survive.

I recount my reactions to two traumatic experiences; and my struggle with anorexia. It is a journey of self-discovery and finding meaning to life. It is a spiritual quest. I share the highs and the lows; the ups and the downs of my life to encourage people in similar situations of grief and loss. I want to tell them to hang in there; if they seek a solution with all their heart they will surely find it.

My original aim in writing was to the Single Parent group, Beulah, connected to St. Mark's church in Dublin. Within this circle I was used to women speaking openly about their frustrations and seeking answers to deep questions. That is why I have been very open about my life in relating my outlook on the single life and the answers I received on how to walk my spiritual journey.

This account of my life relates my reactions to certain people and situations and shows how I worked through those situations. The purpose is not to apportion blame but rather to share how my distorted thinking was straightened out through a gradual healing process.

Rinnah Press
"Menuchah"
Rooghaun, Co.Galway

Origination of Cover by Rinnah Press
Cover Photo: My Childhood Home

ONE

Encounter with God

My story begins in the country, which in my view was the most wonderful place to live. I grew up on a large farm surrounded by woods and trees. There was so much space and so much scope for an active imagination. I played mammies and daddies with my brother Isaac and two sisters Joan and Margaret, setting up a new home almost every week in a different location; either the garden or a corner of the woods. We played cowboys and Indians chasing each other on stick horses across the front field into the haggard field up through Reilly's field or the five-acre field. I kept my distance from the fallow field because of a large stone set at a slight angle up the top left hand corner that looked like a ghost viewing it through the hedge. Dad talked about seeing badgers in that field and because I'd never seen one I connected the badgers with the "ghost"; I thought it might come out to grab me and take me away.

We longed for a real horse to ride; and I was in my teens when Dad's friend loaned Isaac a pony that he shared with his sisters. The pony was very docile and was an asset for learning to ride. It was exciting to mount her and get used to directing her in different manoeuvres. We never had proper riding lessons; we took a few tumbles while we found our way with her. We were going too fast trying to copy the cowboys on television. Once we got used to the pony; I found it was thrilling to ride across the open spaces with the wind blowing in my hair; the freedom was exhilarating.

I was very interested in people and there were a variety of people in my small world to hold my attention. My Dad was a congenial but complex person, nevertheless there was underlying unhappiness, which occasionally came to the surface. My mother was a contented person and very predictable. She was also a peacekeeper. My parents were not demonstrative in their affection for us. My grandmother lived with us; she was another complex individual and unlike my mother was unpredictable. Aunty Mabel lived with us up to the time of her marriage when I was five years old. We loved her and missed her when she left. She was very affectionate and fun to be with; she played the piano and I admired her skill. She played waltzes, marches and hymns on the German piano decorated with brass candlesticks, which was my Grandmother's pride and joy. Aunty Mabel also played the church organ and I aspired to do the same.

And last, but not least, there was Terry who worked for my father. He brought in the cows and milked them daily, and did many other routine jobs about the farm. We pestered him a lot because he liked to talk to us. He had more time for us than our father. And we knew that if we were patient he would share some of his Emerald toffees that he kept in his overcoat pocket. He was the one who shielded us from our parents' knowing the scrapes we got into, like the day Isaac and I played with matches in the cow byre and set the hay in a manger on fire; we thought the byre would burn down and we fled in terror. Later, we crept back only to find that Terry had put the fire out. He gave us an unmerciful scolding that we rightly deserved. It was months later we knew Dad had eventually found out about it but instead of scolding us, surprisingly he teased us about attempting to roast alive one of his cows that was kept in that day because she was sick.

I was sent to boarding school when I was twelve years old; to Preston School in Navan where my two sisters were already boarding; outwardly I got on well enough but inwardly I never settled. I was going on thirteen towards the end of summer term and growing fond of one of the boys; I broke bounds a couple of times to go out with him. My parents took Joan and I out of the school after my first year for financial reasons and sent us to live with Mum's sister. Aunty Frances lived on a farm two miles outside her local town. She was a widow with two children, a son and a daughter. Joan started a secretarial course in the convent while I went into second form. My schoolwork suffered as a result of spending too much time with the local boys. Another year passed and I was sent to a new boarding school, Drewstown House School where my sister Margaret had boarded after leaving Preston. I had been very unhappy with my previous schools, always pining for home.

The day I entered Drewstown I sensed a different atmosphere to the other schools I had attended. The three-storey Georgian house, set in five acres of land with its own lake, was a delightful place. Originally, the school was a mission house for homeless children run under the auspices of "World Missions To Children." Then it was decided in 1964 to start a secondary school and open it to the public. I joined the school in 1966.

On my arrival, the headmistress took me to my dormitory where I found seven other girls busily unpacking their belongings. To my surprise, we each could lay an individual rug on our beds instead of the same coloured spread. The room looked very cosy because a staff member had plaited woolly octopuses and placed them on the beds, and put brightly coloured cushions in the window seats.

After unpacking, we were shown to the Dining room to have supper. I was standing beside the food trolley along with two other girls feeling very nervous, when two boys burst through the door in high spirits. They introduced themselves to us, Eric Foxton and Jack McClintock. They proceeded to tease us as they stuffed themselves with large amounts of bread. The two boys attracted attention by their difference in height. Jack was dwarfed by Eric's tall frame. I was told, later, that they were known as "Jack and the Beanstalk"!

The staff members were warm-hearted, and in Assembly prayers they talked to God as if He was their best friend. The Bible teaching went over my head, but what I enjoyed most about Assembly was the lively gospel hymns that Eric, the Head boy, played on his accordion.

Eric was mischievous and spontaneous, and delighted in challenges. He got the hair-brained idea one Sunday to take us for a different kind of walk. I was all for a novel outing, having come from a boarding school where there was no imagination regarding outings. We just went out walking in two long lines, and never broke out of those lines and we would walk through the town and outside for three to four miles. It was so boring. Can you imagine our surprise when we found Eric was planning to take us through a bog! It was a vast area, very soggy in places. I had come from a farm where we'd lost livestock in the bog, and I had visions of one of us falling down a bog hole, never to be seen again! Once you fell in, you could get sucked down very quickly even with people trying to drag you out.

So we walked as if on eggshells, and crossed many bog holes safely because Eric and one of the staff carried some of the girls on their backs. I wished he had carried me, but no such luck that day! We encountered barbed wire fences and crawled gingerly under them trying not to tear our good Sunday coats! There was a lot of good-natured teasing and laughing along the way. We arrived back at school with a healthy glow on our cheeks from the fresh air and fun we'd enjoyed. We decided we'd better get more appropriate gear when Eric chose that route again.

Eric was gripping my attention for a number of reasons. I had never seen anyone so keen on God before, Eric talked about Him as enthusiastically as swimming and canoeing and all the other things he was interested in. One Saturday he shocked me with some probing questions. We were travelling back to school from an historic field trip in the old boneshaker, a van with rough wooden benches in the back. We were all singing loudly a gospel song, "When the Roll is called up yonder, I'll be there", when suddenly Eric reached over and roared in my ear: "Will you be there?"

"Where?" I asked, surprised.

"To meet the Lord in the air."

I thought he was crazy. I didn't want to think of the words of the song, I just wanted to enjoy the tune. I joined in the singing and ignored Eric, but you couldn't ignore him for long, for he was very persistent.

"Do you know that Jesus is coming back again?"

JESUS IS COMING AGAIN! The thought blew my mind.

Eric explained that the song referred to the end of time when Jesus would return for those whose hearts were ready for him.

I had never heard of such a thing. I was baptized as an infant into the Church of Ireland community. My family had trained me to read the bible and say prayers. It was accepted that this met God's requirements. It was a good basis, and as a child I eagerly read Bible stories about the Patriarchs and the kings and was amazed that some of them ever got mentioned, they were such a bad lot! The account of Jesus' life and death was mostly only mentioned at Christmas and Easter. References to Jesus' coming again were included in one or two prayers, (so I discovered as an adult), but as they were often simply repetition and never expounded upon I missed the point.

I wanted to know how to get ready for Jesus' return. Eric was keen to answer my questions. He had already helped Jack McClintock and some of the other boys to find God. I was told no one knew when Jesus would come back, only God knew, but it was wise to be prepared. The coming of the Lord is spoken of in the Bible as if He's coming very soon. The early Christians lived prepared, believing his coming was imminent. And down through the ages Christians geared themselves for this event, yet He delays His coming. Why is it written as if He might come tomorrow? From my reading of Scripture I see that God's view of time is different to ours, to Him a thousand years is as one day. The coming of the Lord is spoken with urgency to each generation. Each generation needs to be prepared. He gives us time to repent. But now, more than ever before, the event could be closer than we think.

More importantly, is the need to know Jesus as Saviour. Eric wrote notes to me regularly showing me the scriptures about the plan of salvation, repentance and the new birth. Our friends teased us that we were writing love notes but Eric had only one thing on his mind, to get me acquainted with Jesus. Eric presented me with a picture of a Person I really wanted to know, a compassionate and forgiving Lord, who was seeking me out. After all, hadn't He died to save me? This was welcome news, for already in my young life I knew duty to Bible reading and saying prayers did not keep me from falling into temptation. I needed something more. I was conscience stricken over being dishonest about our nights out when I stayed with my Aunt. We told her we were spending the evenings with a neighbour when in reality we were gallivanting about the countryside with the boys.

Added to this was Eric's account of his background. His father had disowned him at the tender age of six months and placed him in a children's home in Dublin. Then he was moved to Drewstown at the age of six. The absence of his mother left him feeling very insecure, and he had a problem with bed wetting until he was fourteen. His encounter with Jesus and subsequent conversion eased the sense of loss.

Eric was eager in his pursuit of God. He spoke a lot about a teacher called John Gray, who had taught in Drewstown for two years and had just moved to Dublin with his wife Joy. John was Eric's mentor in spiritual things, encouraging him to seek after God and to grow in faith. In fact, when Eric met John at first he stuck to him like glue. He admired, so much, John's living faith. So he pestered John continually with questions. Eric's pestering had its lighter side. When John went with some of the boys on holiday to the Isle of Man. One day at teatime, Eric was hyper, talking and teasing continually, so John stood up, grabbed Eric by the scruff of the collar and dragged him outside where he soaked him under a coldwater tap to the amusement of all. It did little to dampen his spirit!

Eric's interest in God drew me and increased my hunger for God. For four months I soaked up all I heard and read, praying earnestly for salvation. From childhood, I had been taught to pray every night, prayers I'd learned off. The prayers were helpful to prompt ideas, but I began to add my own heart prayers at the end. One night, I knew I didn't need to ask any more, I knew something had happened. Everything was fine, God had answered my prayer, and my sense of guilt was gone. I had come in contact with a gracious God who had lovingly drawn me close on that very day. I had chosen to accept Jesus' words on trust. My faith walk had begun.

Now, Eric talked much of the accounts in the book of Acts where the new Christians received the gift of the Holy Spirit and spoke in tongues. It was the expected thing following conversion. Often, Jack joined us in these conversations. It seemed there was an Unseen Presence with us, my faith increased as I listened to Eric speak regularly of the promise of God.

Eric would ask, "Who says religion is boring? It doesn't have to be. Contact with Jesus is the real thing." He was exhilarated by his discoveries in the New Testament. He emphasized commitment to Christ, and then the next vital step was Water Baptism and the Baptism in the Spirit. Eric explained that water baptism or baptism by immersion, was an outward sign of the inward working of salvation, the commitment I had made to Jesus. Going down into the water is identifying oneself with Christ, being buried into His death, and coming up out of the water shows that one is identifying with His resurrection, rising with Christ to new life. I intended to get baptised by immersion as soon as it was practical, but in actual fact I experienced the Baptism in the Spirit first, and then sometime later got baptised in water in Phibsboro Baptist Church in Dublin.

Eric also talked much of developing the use of the gifts of the Spirit. He added, "The gifts of the Spirit should be a part of the regular life of every local church. These supernatural gifts will empower the church to function as God intended. Why is it when God is offering so much, that people settle for so little?" He touched on Jesus' words referring to the fact that his followers should expect to do greater things than He did; because He lives with His Father. Eric asked us, "Can you imagine doing greater works than Jesus? I can hardly wait to get started."[1]

Eric was unpopular with some. Not everybody at Drewstown shared his excitement about the Baptism in the Spirit. It created tension amongst staff and pupils. I could appreciate their difficulty because, at first, when I heard about it, especially speaking in tongues, I had difficulty believing it was possible. Up to that point, it had simply been a story. Pentecost was almost 2,000 years ago. Can you imagine how all this sounded to a curious teenager? The Bible was coming to life; the gifts were not for the early church alone. I was fearful yet deeply interested all at the same time. Church was just a duty up till now, no service stood out from another, but now the central Person within its framework was becoming real to me and I was radical in my actions, even if I was quaking inside. My faith was soon put to the test.

When I prayed about my fears, I came across this verse: "Fear... not, for I am with you: be not dismayed; for I am your God. I will strengthen you, ... I will help you; ... I will uphold you with the right hand of my righteousness."[2] Armed with this large promise it helped me face telling my family what had happened, despite feeling weak at the knees with my heart hammering against my rib cage.

When I went home and shared some of my newfound ideas, my Granny called me a bigot. It stung me, but it was probably deserved, because in my immaturity I said some things without tact. Confirmation classes were soon to be held, and I, like all fourteen year olds within the Church of Ireland, was expected to attend. Eric challenged me about confirmation asking me where the scripture reference was for such action? Having checked it out I didn't feel this was a step I should take; I didn't see any need for it as there was no specific command for it in the Bible. It is a tradition made by man. In my view, believing in Jesus and making a heart commitment to him is all that is necessary for one to receive communion.

When I spoke to my mother about my decision I was so nervous but somehow I blurted the words out and she knew I was serious about the issue. She spoke to our local minister, who advised her to take me away from the school. Mum had no intention of taking me away after the difficulty she had had in finding a suitable school. As she was a very tolerant person she decided to put up with my strong ideas. Fortunately, she had some friends whom she had known from childhood, who used to sing gospel songs around the piano when she visited their home and they talked the same way as me. It stirred memories of when the Spirit of God had touched her and somehow she felt that I was on safe ground. I expected my father to make a scene about confirmation but he never raised the issue. I don't think he was aware of it. My mother was disappointed I would not wear the confirmation veil that my sisters had worn with their school uniform on the day of their confirmation, as tradition dictated.

I didn't expect to receive communion in my home church because of my decision. Instead I had communion at a Pentecostal Church in Dublin, which I had come to attend occasionally. It was only years later, on my return from England, that I attended the Church of Ireland in Co. Westmeath and there the minister wanted to include me at communion, so he spoke to his Bishop and I was given permission to participate.

Despite his enthusiasm for the Baptism in the Spirit, Eric did not receive the gift himself until a few months after he had left school. I asked him what the term "Baptism in the Spirit " meant. Quite simply, he told me the word 'baptism' meant to immerse, as one is immersed or baptised in water. So to be baptized in the Spirit meant to be immersed in the spirit of God. For Eric it was an explosion of joy, a loud, noisy demonstration suited to his character! If it were possible, he was even more voluble in his speaking of this outpouring. His joy was infectious; it stirred such a longing in me for this gift from God.

The following year, while away in Dublin doing a summer job, I spent every spare moment seeking God for this gift. Eric reminded me that the Holy Spirit would make Jesus more real to me and the evidence of speaking in tongues would enrich my spirit and my prayer life. I did not understand really what tongues could do for me. I was nervous about it. Eric and I visited John and Joy's home in Dublin one evening, and before we parted we had a prayer time. It just happened naturally; they were comfortable in God's Presence and entered into a time of praise. I heard them speak in tongues fluently, a language they had never learned, it sounded so beautiful, so perfect, something that was directed entirely to God. It made me long more than ever to experience this gift for myself.

One Sunday evening in a church service, the last hymn challenged me, because I was thirsty in spirit, longing inwardly for God to fill me. There was an increased sense of God's power and an excitement inside me. Something was about to take place. The minister prayed for me, I believed the Holy Spirit was given to me for these words were emphasized: "...how much more shall your Heavenly Father give the Holy Spirit to them that ask Him."[3] But I did not speak in tongues. I was too conscious of people around me.

Eric took me to Howth Hill where we could spend time praying together. But before we knew it I had to rush back to the hostel to avoid being locked out. I didn't have a late key with me. Before I left him, Eric encouraged me to find some place quiet to pray further, to grasp the opportunity God was giving me. As I shared a room, I couldn't pray freely there.

I found a toilet in a quiet corridor, where I reminded myself that God had given me his Spirit, by faith in his promise, all I had to do was speak out in tongues. It was an act of faith. I took a deep breath and started to speak. Strange sounds came out of my mouth, I could have dismissed them as baby talk, gibberish, but I believed God was working in me, and giving me exactly what I asked for, so I persisted. As I continued speaking out the foreign words, I listened, fascinated as my voice raced, with sounds that tumbled over each other. I had no doubt in my heart that I was speaking in tongues. For me it wasn't a big noisy outpouring, but a quiet demonstration that God rewards all who diligently seek him. In the middle of the night, I stirred and whispered words into the pillow to see if I could still do it! Sure enough, the words flowed out of me. God had kept His word; He had freely given me His Holy Spirit.

TWO

To love and to cherish till death us do part
PART I

MY FRIENDSHIP with Eric deepened into love. Love notes passed between us with intense regularity. I was very much attracted to his dynamic personality. He was the life and soul of any gathering. We had a Halloween party at the school. There was the usual excitement planning our fancy dress outfits. I have only a vague recollection of my fancy dress. I think I was the under part of someone else's act. I was padded out with cushions and covers and a girl sat on my shoulders. She was decked out to be a tall, handsome prince. But it was Eric who won the limelight, dressed as a clown in a green outfit with three red pom-poms. Eric kept up steady banter acting like a drunken man, staggering about the place. He sang songs like "Drink to me only with thine eyes", and "Little Brown Jug". He teased my friend, Aisleann *, unmercifully. He loved to find someone who would rise to the occasion and tease him back. Aisleann had a flair for this. Aisleann usually wore her hair in two long plaits. For the party she decided to dress up as a witch, loosening her hair from its bands. She was the envy of all the girls as we admired her beautiful long, brown tresses.

It came as a surprise to me that Eric chose someone quite his opposite to marry. He even gave up a girl he had been quite fond of, to develop a relationship with me. She was working in a children's home, and sounded like a very competent girl. Surely she would have suited him better. Eric said she was a lovely girl, but she was not the Lord's choice for him. Secretly I wondered what he saw in me. This was when I was assailed with self-doubt. I knew his hopes and aspirations, and sometimes doubted that I could truly support him in them. He said to me "You are quiet and thoughtful. And I like your inquisitive mind about God." Just before he left the school, he confided to me that we would marry one day! I wondered how he could be so sure. He talked in that trusting way about an impression the Holy Spirit was giving him. For two years, our relationship was spasmodic with odd letters written, and occasionally meeting together in Dublin. Once I was out of school I headed for the city to be with Eric. He worked for an engineering company and studied a course to further his chances in the job, while he followed his goal to become a minister in his spare time, and I held an office job while studying music in the evenings. I worked in RTV Rentals in the Head Office, first as a copy typist and then as an NCR operator. It was a very mundane job; I looked on it as a means to earn money until I qualified as a music teacher.

The first time I took Eric home to the farm I showed him over the whole house. I told him I loved this house so much, that every time I returned home I would go into all the rooms just to savour the pleasure of being home again. I loved the spacious reception rooms with the big fireplaces and high ceilings.

(I didn't like the fireplaces in the bedrooms because of my fear of the dark and sometimes I wondered if something evil was lurking up the chimney.) I recalled pleasant childhood memories of when the house echoed with our noise and laughter and Mum would call us down to dinner and we would dash out on the landing and slide down the long banisters. For Eric, listening to this account, there was a fleeting thought of his parents' farmhouse and the pain of not being allowed to grow up there.

We went through the five bedrooms and the old playroom, finishing up in the Dining Room where there was a large bookcase in one corner, the total sum of our supply of books. Eric examined the books with interest. On the lower shelves were old novels of Annie S. Swan, that my mother loved, History books, Poetry and Children's books. Eric loved books and was attempting to build up a Library of autobiographies, Bible commentaries, and concordances. Every birthday, and Christmas he would suggest a title of a book he was interested in hoping I would buy it for him. Often he would browse in second-hand bookshops to get the books he wanted for study. He reached to see the books on the top shelves. There were old religious books up there gathering dust, He took one old book with it's cover partly torn. He made an exclamation of joy; it was a volume of C.H. Spurgeon's sermons. Eric was delighted, for he admired the works of this 19th century preacher. He had already collected some of his books.

Eric acted as if he had found gold dust amongst the old books. He was thumbing through the book to see the contents. As he was so excited and interested, I suggested we sit in the study and he could take a closer look. We nestled close together in an armchair, and read together and discussed one of those sermons. The time flew by, as we were absorbed in the subject.

He was gathering ideas for next Sunday's sermon. Afterwards, Eric remarked: "See, what other girl would sit and humour me for an hour or more over an old dusty book. You have the same appreciation for books, that's another reason why I love you!"

It was understood that we would marry when I reached 21, but Eric had a strong impression to make plans for our wedding around my nineteenth birthday. As it happened, if there had been a delay, there would have been no wedding! Our friends teased Eric about his child-bride, and the cook in the Hostel where I now lived, declared that Eric was "Cradle-snatching"!

Then there was the matter of obtaining my father's written permission as I was under age, to get a marriage licence. Dad welcomed Eric because Eric fitted in so easily with life on the farm. I remember the day that Eric climbed the hill in the five-acre field, where Dad was making hay. I sat on the five-barred gate watching the scene. Eric called out to Dad, Dad turned in his direction, laid down the hayfork and taking off his straw hat wiped the perspiration from his brow. Eric held out the form and Dad duly signed on the dotted line, then they spat on the palms of their hands and shook hands warmly, as if they had just transacted a business deal over some cattle!

When we planned our wedding, I would sometimes shop in town on a Saturday for my trousseau. Headlines in the newspapers would catch my eye. Another person shot to death in the North. The troubles had been brewing for two years now. And I wondered; as I walked from shop to shop, how long would peace continue? Would it remain quiet in the South? Could we be sure of shopping in safety on our streets? Would the troubles erupt into a full-scale civil war? The political climate affected my outlook. What did the future hold for Eric and I, and the family we hoped to rear? Would the lives of our children be overshadowed by war?

Our Wednesday night prayer meetings were focused on this and the spiritual condition of our country. There was a sense of excitement and expectancy in these meetings. There were some dear old ladies who came from other churches to join us and they prayed with great energy for Ireland, they were travailing in prayer. To look at them they were frail physically, but spiritually they were as strong as an ox! We learned much from their example.

After leaving Drewstown, Eric had helped an ex Congo missionary and John Gray start a small Pentecostal Church in Lower Gardiner Street, Dublin. At the opening meeting of our small church that was in basement premises, a visiting speaker gave a prophetic sermon. This word focused our prayer life for the future. It was taken from the story where the prophet Elisha told the kings of Israel and Judah to make trenches and the valley would be filled with water without the aid of wind or rain. It would be an easy thing for God to perform. They would have enough water for the army to drink and to water the animals. The two kings were in the desert on their way to fight the king of Moab who was rebelling against them. The kings and their armies ran out of water. They called on Elisha to enquire from God what they should do. And so Elisha gave them the instructions.[1] We wondered what we could learn from this as a church? Ireland was an extremely parched land at that time, badly in need of refreshing. We were instructed to make trenches to hold Heaven's supply to water a thirsty nation. We were told that it would be hard work, praying, like digging in the heat of the day. But suddenly, there would be a flood of blessing. If people were faithful they would have lots to share.

Over the next few years there was continuous "digging" in

the prayer meetings. Gradually, there was a change; people came from the Quaker meetings thirsty for the blessing of God. A priest and his students, from Maynooth College, turned up at our meetings, something unheard of, they too were seeking for greater blessing. One of the student priests began to come frequently, and his eyes would shine as he discussed spiritual things with Eric.

One Sunday, he accompanied us down the country, stopping for a picnic on the way. In a house meeting we sang gospel songs and Eric preached convincingly the truths of salvation. It was noted that the young priest was very absorbed. Back in Dublin, in the evening meeting, he was asked to share and Eric felt that while he spoke he fought his way into the kingdom. He was struggling because of the way he had been brought up to approach God and now he was being shown this liberating approach. It was as if he had a revelation as he spoke and by the time he had finished, he had embraced the freedom of Christ.

By this time, Eric was getting opportunities to speak around the country. He encouraged everyone he met to search for God and the gift of his Holy Spirit. When he prayed for them, inevitably they received the Holy Spirit.

Noel Macfarlane, an elder in the church, had a great experience. There were plans afoot for Eric, Noel and others to go down the country and attend open airs in two areas. Eric asked Noel, in advance, to share his story at the open air. Margaret, Noel's wife, begged him not to speak where he was well known, but Noel didn't let that stop him. When the moment came to speak at the open air, he was afraid and his legs felt like jelly, but when he started sharing he felt a great joy and it carried him through.

Coming home in the van, over the Dublin Mountains; Eric

and Noel were talking in the back and Eric asked if Noel would like to receive the Baptism in the Spirit. Over the past months, Eric had visited Noel and Margaret's house regularly; and they had great discussions that would turn into arguments at times. Margaret was very hungry and would ask Eric back again and again. Now, Noel said, "Yes" because he knew he was ready. Eric shouted to the driver "Stop the van. We're going to pray." They prayed on the side of the road. Noel was bursting with joy when he received the Baptism and spoke in tongues.

He was on "cloud nine" at home, so much so, that he would speak in tongues in his sleep. Margaret would be annoyed with him waking her in the middle of the night, so she'd whack him with her slipper to stop him! She went to the senior pastor and asked what could be done. He assured her that Noel would settle down in a couple of weeks, it was just the newness and thrill of the experience that was causing the nightly disturbance. Sure enough, Noel had quietened down, but the experience had such an effect upon his life that Margaret soon came into the blessing.

Margaret's mother objected strongly to the church they were attending, and the young pastor's preaching. Noel would defend Eric and say; "Don't speak against the Lord's anointed." The blessing that had come to Noel and Margaret spilled over to their family and Margaret's mother repented, was converted and also baptised in the Holy Spirit.

Eric was now the full time pastor of our small church. He devoted his time to Bible study, prayer and visitation. Plans were going ahead for our wedding. Eric invited his parents to the wedding, but they didn't come. For a time, his father had shown some interest in him after he left school, so Eric went home to live with them. His father noticed Eric's love of music, and bought him a brand new accordion. He was very proud of him as Eric played it for his friends in the local pub, but when Eric took it to play in open-air meetings back in the city, his father was furious and took the accordion away from him. He never saw it again. His father was a very bitter man; he cut Eric off at that point, and as a consequence Eric lost his inheritance. His father owned a large farm. This was a second rejection from his father in his young life and very distressing, for he knew his mother loved him and he found it hard to bear the separation. Eric's Dad had disowned him because he stated emphatically that he was not his son. Eric was born seven months after his parents had married; his father believed Eric was another man's child.

Eric's Aunts, on his mother's side, told me they were convinced Eric was Tom Foxton's son; because as an adult he resembled his father so much. When Eric moved to Dublin he was keen to visit the Customs House, with John, to get a copy of his birth certificate. He was hoping to find his father's name on the document. It devastated him to find there was no name under 'father'. Eric was so grateful for John's support that dreadful day, just to help him come to terms with the situation.

The subject was never discussed when I visited Mum Foxton following Tom's death. I think it was very sad that Eric was displaced because they never had any more children. Eric knew he was losing a lot in terms of his earthly inheritance, but from an eternal perspective he believed he would receive a far greater inheritance.

Despite this sadness, once we were married, Eric continued to share with people, as opportunities arose, the relevance of the Bible for today, and to encourage them to search for God. It

To love and to cherish until death us do part – Part One

was not surprising that even on our honeymoon Eric couldn't resist the request from a friend to pray together. We were staying in Glengariff, West Cork, and drove to Emily's * home in time for dinner. After a substantial traditional Irish meal, we went for a drive, with Eric and Emily talking animatedly about the Holy Spirit. She was longing for more of God. On a quiet road, Eric parked the car and we prayed together. Emily was greatly blessed that day, as Eric laid hands on her head and asked God to give His gift of the Holy Spirit. On our return to the house, our little hired mini fairly bounced along, Eric was that euphoric over the favour and leading of the Lord in Emily's life. Today, she still radiates the joy of the Lord, and blesses many through her intercessory prayers.

We moved into a one room flat in Blackrock, renting from Christian friends. Shortly after we moved in, the family went on holiday and we had the use of the kitchen with the cosy Aga stove and the piano in the sitting room for almost a month. Then we heard that the house next door to John and Joy was up for sale. We couldn't afford to buy it but unexpectedly, we were given the opportunity to live there while the sale was in process. The owner had already bought another house and wanted to move in, when he heard Eric was in need of a place to stay, he agreed to let us stay. The most unexpected thing was he wouldn't accept any rent because he had respect for priests and seeing Eric was a minister he classed him in the category of a priest. Ten months later, Noel's brother, Bertie, bought the house as an investment and rented it to us. Bertie blessed us so much in this respect.

Our door was always open to people. We had visitors over to dinner most Sundays and people in need within the church came to stay from time to time. There were a number of occasions when Christian workers from other churches brought needy people to us; some stayed longer than others depending on their circumstances. When you live closely with others for a certain length of time it usually shows up areas in our lives that we're not aware of; these were periods of adjustment where we sought to learn tolerance and forbearance.

We were married for about five months when I noticed a slight strain come into my relationship with Eric. On my part, there were early signs of repressed feelings. In our partnership, Eric did most of the talking while I listened. He told me I was a good listener and when I asked, once, did he think that I was too quiet, he replied, "Still waters run deep." He thought that I had deep thoughts to share. I wonder what he would have thought if I'd told him some of my fears, how I didn't feel equal to the task of being a pastor's wife. If I were to mention it I'd be told, "but you have God to help you." Yes, I knew that but somehow it didn't help enough with the unease inside of me. I was a mixture of faith and fear. I didn't know my own strengths. I was more aware of the fears. In one way, I was independent, for years at boarding school had made me so. I had to find a way to survive. I looked like I had it all together, that I could cope with life's challenges. But inside myself, I was very insecure. Eric's faith and hope would usually chase my blues away quite quickly. One thing he observed about me, that I was a fussy eater and prone to diets. He'd say that I looked fine, he liked me the way I was, he didn't think I needed to lose weight. It wasn't enough for me. I couldn't make him understand.

Eric had a great capacity to love and to be open. Having to deal with his father's rejection in his young life had caused him to plumb the depths of God's love and so he loved people with a passion, including me, which tended to overwhelm me at times. I wasn't used to love on this scale. It invited an openness that I was unable to respond to in full. Even though I had taken some dramatic steps at the start of my conversion, I came up against some blockages within me that I couldn't explain which prevented me moving easily with the Holy Spirit's leading.

I discovered I was pregnant in an odd way. During our first Christmas together, I had a severe bout of influenza, which left me feeling very low. After about three weeks, I was still in bed and feeling wretched. In exasperation, we consulted the doctor once again, and this time he told me I was pregnant. I remember Eric and John laughing when the diagnosis was made. John remarked, "It's the first time I heard pregnancy described as flu." It was a relief to everyone to know the cause of my illness, and naturally I was pleased I was having a baby. It was what Eric and I both wanted. When we first got married, we talked about having a baby in about two years. Some months after, we decided we wanted one sooner; this was providential because if we had kept to our first decision there would have been no baby.

But now that I was pregnant for real, I felt so ill it clouded my joy. It was a jolt to find that the pleasure of a baby coming could cause such mixed feelings. I was very sick and very depressed although I didn't admit this; I felt it wouldn't do for a pastor's wife to admit she was depressed. It just seemed such an effort to try to get up and live my day. What I had been told to expect regarding pregnancy was possibly morning sickness and strange cravings in the early months. So I was very much taken by surprise to find myself sick most of the day for months on end; and the last place I wanted to be was in the kitchen cooking dinner. There was also an underlying problem that I couldn't separate from all the changes taking place at that time. It caused friction in our marriage. Thankfully, during the last three months I began to feel normal again and started to thrive.

Two months before our first anniversary Eric applied for, and obtained a job as a sales rep selling office equipment, to supplement his income. While Eric was adjusting to his new job, I prepared for the birth of our baby, supported by Joy who was also expecting her third child. I heard a story about Pauline, John and Joy's three-year-old daughter. John had explained about the new baby growing inside Joy, and Pauline was working it all out in her little mind. One breakfast time, watching her mother eating porridge, Pauline exclaimed, "Oh, the porridge is going all over the baby. Yuck!" The baby was born in March, unspoiled by the porridge, and was named Leslie. I had a golden opportunity to practise for the birth of my baby; I had some fun times feeding and bathing Leslie.

Three events stand out from this period. The first took place in July, one month before the baby's birth. The milkman doing his rounds one Saturday at about 4 a.m wakened us. He seemed extra noisy that day for some reason. We talked awhile, and seeing we were so wide awake, Eric decided to go downstairs to his office to pray. I followed, not to pray, but to look for a book on his bookshelf. I picked up a book by a woman who had lost her husband. It was apparent she had suffered a great shock and immense sadness; it seems she experienced a supernatural strength in the days following her husband's death. This story made a great impression on me, as I was about to find out before too long.

The second thing worth noting was the day that Eric bought a record of a male voice choir, and he used to get taken up with the songs on it, especially one particular song that made reference to seeing Jesus face to face. One Saturday, I was busy baking for visitors coming to dinner the next day I could hear the record playing in the sitting room. Once I had finished clearing up I went to join Eric, I opened the door to the sitting room to find him standing in the middle of the room with his hands raised and a glow on his face. He was totally absorbed in the song as if Jesus stood right before him. Quietly I shut the door and returned to the kitchen, pondering over what I had just witnessed.

It reminded me of one Wednesday Bible study, where Eric was teaching from the verse "For...me, to live is Christ and to die is gain."[2] While Eric expounded on his favourite theme, I had the strangest feeling while watching him, he looked like his spirit was ready to burst out and take flight to higher realms to be with the Lord he loved so much. I felt we were worlds apart when it came to worship. I did not know what Eric experienced and I envied him. Also, I knew that he had often expressed his longing to see the Lord but I could not share his present involvement.

The third event was brief and puzzling. We were having a coffee break one afternoon, talking in a desultory manner, when Eric remarked, "If I died, I'd hope you would get married again. I wouldn't like you to be on your own." Treating it casually, but not caring very much for the conversation, I listened to him rambling on about the eligible men in the church. I laughed at his suggestions and then told him to shut up, adding," I'm very happy with the man I've got, thank you very much." He didn't press his point; he just reached out for me and held me close. Needless to say, I was baffled at his words, and decided to push them to the back of my mind.

It Happened Again

On the morning of our first wedding anniversary, 14th August 1972, Eric set out for Co. Cavan, promising me that he would be back in time to celebrate our anniversary meal. The original plan was to travel together and spend the night in some hotel, but our plan was foiled. Two days before, there were signs that the baby could be born very soon. In fact, it was a miracle I didn't die too or suffer serious injuries, as I had planned to go with Eric. If I hadn't heeded the warning I would have surely come to grief.

During the day, cards and flowers arrived from family and friends for our anniversary. At 5p.m. I was baking a special cake when the doorbell rang once again. I was enjoying the expression of love shown by the family, and longing for Eric to get back and enjoy it with me, but it was a little early for Eric to arrive and he would have his own key. I got the shock of my life when I opened the door to find a tall Guard standing there urging me to phone Cavan Hospital, that my husband had been involved in an accident.

Left alone, I walked around the house in a daze, weeping hysterically. The idea of Eric lying injured in some strange hospital bed disturbed me terribly; he was always so strong and in control. I leaned on him for support when trouble arose, now I felt completely adrift. It took me about half-an-hour to grow calm enough to go next door to John and Joy and make the phone call, not having a phone of our own at the time. When I got through to the Matron at the Hospital, she told me that Eric was critically ill and asked if I could get to the hospital as soon as possible. I felt so weak and unable to speak. Because I didn't reply forever so long, she spoke loudly and firmly repeating the urgency to come soon. I tried again to speak, but my words were not coherent, I was trembling so much, then I was aware of Joy coming to my side and gently taking the phone to get details.

I was sitting in a daze on the settee when Joy suggested I go home to pack an overnight bag while she and John rushed around to arrange a babysitter for their children. Once we were on the road, questions raced around my head: "What if he's dead? No, no, he couldn't die, oh no, he must not die! What would the church do without him? What would I do without him? How could I live without his laughter and love.... I need him so much." And so it went on. Fear and panic gripped my heart. It was only about 65 miles to Cavan, yet it seemed the longest journey I ever had to endure.

We waited in the Matron's office for ten long minutes, and then she came and sat holding my hand as she broke the news that Eric had died just half an hour before our arrival. I turned to Joy and wept in her arms. Then suddenly I stemmed the tide of my emotion for some unknown reason. Inwardly I thought: "If only I had not lost control at home, a precious half hour that would have meant getting to the Hospital in time to say 'goodbye.' Why, oh why, didn't I get a grip on myself and make that telephone call earlier?"

But it wouldn't have made any difference, for Eric had never regained consciousness since his arrival in the hospital, from fractures he had sustained to his head and chest as the result of colliding with a timber lorry on a hazardous bend on the Cavan/Butlersbridge Road. With a blow like this, the bottom had fallen out of my world. We had so much going for us - expecting our first baby, a good home, family and friends, a young church that held such promise, and openings further a field for Eric to speak. All that time and effort he spent studying and praying, talking with people one to one, was it all to come to nothing? Why was our life so rudely interrupted?

It just didn't bear thinking about, how could this happen? Eric was gone! He was only 23 years old. Death had snatched him away so suddenly. We had been married exactly one year to the day, and I was pregnant and feeling very vulnerable. How was I going to manage? While I thought such forlorn thoughts, another thought cut across my thinking: MY THOUGHTS ARE NOT YOUR THOUGHTS.[3] I recognized the Holy Spirit speaking. He seemed to be saying that I was seeing this event from a human perspective but He saw it from a different perspective. He was asking me to trust him, even though everything seemed black. I didn't understand, but it was like a lifeline. I headed for the ward to say my final farewell to Eric.

The matron and Joy were anxious for me going to see Eric; they feared I might go into emergency labour. But I needed so much to see him one last time. We walked endless corridors, or so it seemed, to get to the ward. I entered the ward and looked around; life was continuing for everybody else, but for me, for these moments at least, time stood still. The matron guided me to the bed in the corner nearest the door and pulled a screen around the bed. I looked at my young husband lying so still on the bed. As I kissed his cheek, I had the unmistakable sense that Eric's spirit had left; he was already in the Presence of God. I was in a state of awe and wonder. At that moment, I really couldn't object, for I knew he longed so much for God.

It was faith and trust in God that upheld me that day, the seed of which Eric had planted in my young life some years before. It gave me courage to plan and attend his funeral. During the service, as we sang the hymn, "Thine be the Glory, risen conquering Son," I could picture Jesus standing amongst us, dispelling fear, offering me hope for the future despite the circumstances. A pastor from the North who had encouraged Eric a lot in his ministry, chose as his text, "You do not realize now what I am doing, but later you will understand." [4] As I walked away from the grave, seeing the crowds that had come to pay their respects, I had the inexplicable urge to talk to Eric about it all. He was loved so dearly, if only he knew how many had turned out to say farewell to him. I think it was heartbreaking to realise that Eric, who had been a homeless boy, and had looked forward to being a father so much would never see his newborn baby.

Yet Eric had long been caught up in the greater scheme of things; he had been very focused on eternal things. Now, he was <u>in</u> eternity. His delight in God had been so obvious. His joyous nature was very infectious, while visiting members of his congregation he would have them laughing and relaxing very quickly in his company. As I reflected on this, I wondered what it must have been like for him to pass from this world to the next. I would have loved a glimpse of his entrance into heaven. Knowing him, he must have caused quite a stir! I'd say he set out to explore his new surroundings with all the enthusiasm of a holidaymaker sightseeing. He was now face to face with Jesus, the One he had admired so much. I'm sure his joy knew no bounds, basking in the sunshine of His love. It just boggles the mind. We are told that there is great joy in the Presence of God, and lasting pleasures.[5] I thought, if Eric enjoyed God so much here on earth, then I figured that he would continue to do so in Heaven where God's Presence would be felt in greater measure, and those pleasures would be presented on a vast, extended scale.

I thought of his last sermon that was based on these words, "We have escaped like a bird out of the fowler's snare; the snare has been broken, and we have escaped."[6] The context of the Psalm is the struggle the believer experiences when he breaks free from the forces of darkness. For Eric it was ultimately a physical break from the trappings of mortality, and he was now as free as a bird in the glory of heaven.

In the following days, I felt as if I walked upon holy ground, even with the birth of my daughter, Esther, born the day after the funeral. Esther's coming gave me something to live for, I was so thankful to have her as a reminder of her father. As I rested in the hospital, I had a sense of God's Presence that awed me greatly. I remembered the story of the woman losing her husband; and the unusual strength that sustained her through the early days of bereavement. I found this was my experience too; the comfort of God was like a cushion-protection from the awful blow that had befallen me.

Even to hear that I had failed the practical for a Diploma in music didn't bother me unduly; I had passed the theory section and now I had a chance to repeat the practical section within the next year. After spending six weeks with family and friends, I returned home to continue my studies and to give piano lessons in my home as a source of income. Within a few weeks of distributing leaflets around our housing estate and beyond, I had about twenty-four pupils coming each week including Mark, John and Joy's six-year-old son.

I received many cards and letters offering sympathy and love. Many people enclosed generous cheques, and there were a great many parcels containing baby clothes. I think Esther had enough outfits to clothe her for the next two years!

It meant a lot to me that Eric and I had chosen names for the baby. For months, Eric playfully named the "bump", Habakkuk, simply because it was an outrageous Bible name for an infant! We were both drawn to certain Bible names because of the manner in which some parents chose names for their offspring that would be an indication to their character or purpose in life. We thought a great deal about it and finally settled for Nathaniel (Eric's middle name) if it was a boy, and Esther if it was a girl. I think it was more the character of Queen Esther, than the meaning of her name; that we wished to be evident in our daughter as she grew up. Queen Esther is portrayed in Scripture as a brave, unselfish person who intercedes at a time of crisis for her people.[7]

Esther's birth was like a dream. It seemed to be happening at a distance from me, because I was so drugged I felt no pain at all. It was like moving through a mist, then bright lights blinding me, then nothing but darkness, then bright lights again. A voice was shouting from far away, "push, push", I tried to push but seemed to be paralysed. Then somebody called out, "It's a girl." But I forgot and asked over and over about the baby. It was the next morning at feeding time that I saw my daughter for the first time, as she was wheeled into the private ward given to me at the last minute due to the extenuating circumstances. I was told later that Esther's birth was a forceps delivery. Forceps are, in effect, large sugar tongs used to speed up the birth of the baby. The staff tried to spare me any undue stress. The marks of the tongs showed on her head for weeks after, but Esther suffered no ill effects.

Esther was a quiet baby, feeding at regular intervals and she slept a lot. As she got older, I placed her in her baby chair near the piano while I instructed my pupils. (I think some of it rubbed off on her, for today Esther enjoys playing the piano.)

It Happened Again

For all the joy of having my little girl, and being very busy in the daytime, yet sometimes in the evening while Esther lay sleeping in her cot, I would stand gazing at her, a lump forming in my throat and wonder what was the matter with me. Somewhere deep inside I wanted to cry but couldn't. I could not love my baby as I wanted to, I didn't dote freely over her, talk to her as other mothers did. I guess the natural reaction was to want Eric to be with me to enjoy our baby together. But there was no release of tears, not since the day the Matron had told me the news of Eric's death.

The glory that surrounded me at the funeral had faded. There was a tight feeling inside my chest that I could not handle.

I received many cards and letters from friends especially one from our former pastor. He wrote about a verse that had struck him, forcibly, regarding Eric's life.[8] It referred to the analogy of a grain of wheat – if it falls to the ground and dies (is planted) it creates many seeds. If it isn't put in the ground it will not multiply. The picture conveyed to me that Eric's life and ministry were not wasted. His death would yield many seeds. And this is what happened. The challenge of his life was similarly reflected in the lives of others with whom he had contact. Indeed I received letters from people who had been so impressed by his life that they had rededicated their lives to God. One person made a decision to be a missionary.

I thought a lot about the experience of loss and focused on the life of Job over this period. I had first read about this long-suffering Bible character when I was sixteen. Up to this point I was only familiar with the expression, "the patience of Job" or "Job's comforters". His story made a great impression on me. Now the thoughts came flooding back to me. Job was a man

To love and to cherish until death us do part – Part One

who had suffered great calamity. I was fascinated with the account of his life. We are given a glimpse behind the scenes in heaven, in connection with events carried out on earth. It was incredible how Satan had the audacity to appear before God and talk in such a manner! Satan dared to say to the Almighty, "Does Job fear God for nothing?"[9] The cheek of him! He was implying that Job feared God only because of the benefits he received. I was struck by the fact that God had a hedge around Job. Then God allowed that hedge to be removed, and Satan was able to touch his family and his property. Satan could only go as far as God permitted. Twice God cautioned Satan not to lay a finger on Job. It was later that God gave permission to Satan to strike Job with illness. I wondered if God had removed the hedge from around Eric, even allowing Satan to touch his life, which I thought was a very severe thing, to test me.

I felt that one of the girls at the office, where I had worked, had thrown out the same challenge to me that Satan had used concerning Job. "Does Job fear God for nothing?" Lisa* and I worked together on the same NCR (National Cash Register) machine. I had trained her into the job. Like most girls we discussed many subjects, especially boyfriends. I was engaged to Eric at the time, and naturally, there was a lot of talk concerning wedding plans. Because God was part and parcel of my life, He slipped easily into the conversation. Lisa was very curious and asked many questions about my faith. She was going through great difficulty as the result of a motorcycle accident where she and her boyfriend had crashed and one of her legs was badly injured. She had had many operations and wore a calliper to support her leg. For a time, work was very pleasant as we enjoyed these friendly discussions. In a practical way, Lisa offered to help my wedding plans forward by offering to make a bridesmaid's dress for my sister, Margaret, in green satin.

A noticeable change came in our discussions when Lisa talked one morning about how easy it was for me to trust in God for I had everything. According to her, I had good health, I was getting married, and the future was rosy. She couldn't get married because she needed to have more operations on her leg. Her life was interrupted by one operation after another. And it took the leg so long to heal each time. It was so difficult for her to remain even-tempered in such an uncertain and painful situation. My heart went out to her.

When I returned to work after our honeymoon, I heard that Lisa was in hospital, so I went along to visit her. The visit didn't go well, the conversation was strained. The distance between us was too great in Lisa's eyes. My happiness made things uncomfortable. I tried to understand her position. What could I say? I left the hospital feeling very sad for my friend. Oh, dear Lisa, if you only knew how soon my life was to be overshadowed by great tragedy and heartache! Only one year away and I would be faced with incalculable loss.

When tragedy struck, I maintained that God had a purpose in it all, even though it was surely a very dramatic and costly purpose. I also believed that God ordains our days.[10] The date and the circumstances of our death are in His keeping. Therefore, to my way of thinking, what happened was in God's control. This was the anchor that kept me focused. Without it, it would seem I was at the mercy of a very malignant spirit.

I recalled a scrap of conversation during tea break with the girls at work some months after I got married, how one talked about her husband in the Garda Siochana and hoped that nothing dreadful would ever happen to him. Somebody asked me, "If your husband died, what would you do?" I replied, "I think

I'd want to die too." Left to myself that's what I would want to do, now that it had happened. But God in his love had stepped in to give me faith and courage, and I had a baby daughter dependent on me. I had to bear up if only for her sake.

Eric had a warning about his death. One day in the summer of 1970, he had a premonition or forewarning that someone was going to die. It was slightly different from the usual premonition in that Eric was used to receiving prophetic insight in a church context, as were other members of the congregation; to share what God showed him with the people, usually to encourage and build them up. He hesitated to share it because of its delicate nature.

He sought counsel from his pastor, and from John Gray. The pastor encouraged him to share it if the Holy Spirit prompted him. As John listened to the content, a feeling of dread came over him, which greatly puzzled him. Eventually Eric did share the warning in a public service, never guessing that it was referring to himself.

He had another warning in 1972, a few months before his death, at an elder's meeting in Noel Macfarlane's home. He said, "God is taking something away from you...." On the way home John said to Eric, "You should have said 'someone', not 'something', shouldn't you?" Eric replied, "Yes," John had that feeling of dread again. John felt it was someone in his family, possibly his son, Mark, who had asthmatic attacks and one night he had had to be taken to hospital for oxygen. After Eric's death, John knew why the warning had caught his attention; Eric had become part of his family circle renting a room from him for about two years. John and Eric had grown close over the years. Somehow, to have been forewarned helped us all, the event had not happened at random.

It Happened Again

I believe now that Eric, because he'd been alerted twice, was preparing me that day he spoke to me of dying, just in case he was the one to be taken. That summer, John and Eric had an unexpected conversation. John and Joy had been on holiday in England. They had left their white canary, which the children called Snowy, with us. When they returned, John crossed over the wall in his back garden to collect the bird and stood talking to Eric who was weeding his vegetable plot. They got talking about the future. John said he could see nothing but difficulty and heartache ahead, while Eric said that to him the future looked really glorious. John was struck by the contrast in their views. Eric didn't realise that he was looking at Heaven! In a matter of weeks his life was cut short, he was gone to discover this glorious future.

(* Names of certain people have been changed to protect their privacy.)

‧⁃ THREE ⁃‧

To love and to cherish till death us do part
PART II

During the next year, I started corresponding with Eddy Bowen whom I had met at my sister's wedding in Walton-on-the-Naze, Essex. For us, it was instant attraction, as we almost collided on the steps leading to our holiday flat. When Esther was six weeks old, I went with my parents and brother to play the piano at my sister Margaret's wedding. It was something that Eric and I had arranged months before with Margaret. My friends wondered would it be too emotional for me to take part in the service so soon after Eric's death. I didn't want to disappoint Margaret so kept to the plan.

We arrived in Walton at 4.30 am, on the morning of the wedding! Our adventure in Dad's old Austin Cambridge breaking down on the M6 and M1 was a nightmare, and delayed us two days. But that is almost a story in itself. I had just slept one and a half hours when Esther cried for her 6a.m. feed. After that it was all go with preparations for the wedding. I was told that

It Happened Again

Esther and I would be driven to the church in the best man's car when he came to collect the bridegroom. I thought this was very funny, knowing the best man's duty was to look after the bridegroom. Margaret told me there was loads of room in the boot of his estate car to carry Esther's pram. I thought this was a ridiculous idea, that was, until I met the best man!

Feeling muzzy from lack of sleep, and looking very dishevelled, my arms weighed down with my baby daughter, towels, and changing pad, I hurried back from Margaret's flat where I'd bathed Esther and ran into Eddy on the outside steps of our flat. He loomed large above me. Wow, this fellow was really tall. I thought that Eric was tall at six foot, but Eddy was at least four inches taller again. My future brother-in-law introduced us. Eddy smiled disarmingly and I was drawn to him.

Eddy was pastor of the A.O.G. (Assembly of God) church in the small seaside town. He had a practical love for God, enjoying children's clubs, beach missions and Sunday school telling stories and playing action songs on his guitar. He had a flair for telling jokes, and imitating Donald Duck and other voices of Walt Disney characters! Eddy was born in India, the son of missionaries. His father came from Herefordshire, England and his mother came from Turku, Finland. They met in India while studying the language on the mission field. Eddy's Mum told me that he was lapping up Indian curry before the age of one, because everyone loved the white baby, and when Eddy learned to crawl from house to house, they shared their meal with him! As a child Eddy was very affectionate, he used to say to his mother, "I love you from earth to heaven and from heaven to earth." He wanted so much to put his love into words yet he couldn't measure it so this was his way of expressing it.

I felt drawn to Eddy the more we corresponded, he planned

to come to Ireland to get better acquainted with me. My mother, who had seen Eddy give Esther a lot of attention at my sister's wedding, matched us up straightaway and when she heard that he had sent me a Christmas card she thought things were very hopeful. Very soon we kept the postmen busy writing letters twice a week. I was totally unprepared when his seventh letter contained a poem and a proposal of marriage!

> God's way, though strange at times to human mind
> Is best,
> His love for us is tender, pure, and kind,
> In Him alone my soul finds perfect rest.
> "I will meet all your needs," we hear Him say
> So clear,
> We know, as we stay with Him day by day
> He clothes us, feeds us - we have nought to fear.
> Our ways were brought together - not by chance-
> The Lord
> Gave us a spark of love that must advance
> And grow - He'll lead us by His mighty Word.

The proposal was unexpected, but not unwelcome. To me our meeting was very much directed by God. I had not sought love or marriage, but certainly the 'spark of love' had advanced.

Meanwhile Eddy decided to take time out from the pastoral work to spend a year in the A.O.G. Home Missions programme to help in evangelistic outreach in Wales. Eddy felt he had given all he could give to the people in Walton. He had spent two years in I.B.T.I. (International Bible Training Institute) and gone straight into pastoral work at the age of nineteen. Having spent a further two years as pastor he wanted a change. I was rather disappointed. The pastoral work was familiar ground to me, but I lacked experience in outreach. I wasn't sure how I could support Eddy in this venture. I wanted him to be happy and if it meant moving to Wales then I would agree to go, I didn't want him to feel trapped in his work in Walton.

When Eddy was due to come over on the boat in May '73, my mother wanted to help the course of true love run smoothly, and said she would drive me out to meet the boat at 6.30a.m. True to her word, she turned up the night before in the old Austin. Next morning, we were up at 5.30a.m dressing and feeding Esther. I could hardly contain my excitement. The plan was that Mum would drop me off to spend time with Eddy, who was bringing his own car, and Mum would take Esther to the farm where we would all meet up later for lunch. The Austin didn't let us down this time; we arrived in Dun Laoghaire just as the boat was about to dock.

Once the boat had docked, Eddy's car was one of the first to drive off. He found a parking space quickly, and we walked on to the pier, found a bench overlooking the rocks. Eddy took a small box from his pocket and handed it to me. It contained an engagement ring with three stones, two diamonds and a sapphire in the centre! This was a great surprise. I expected that we would go shopping for a ring together during Eddy's visit; I never thought he'd choose the ring himself. He must have been very confident that I would like it. Of course I liked it. I appreciated the gesture and treasured this romantic moment by the sea. It was a great feeling to be in love with somebody again.

Eddy was so comfortable to talk with and later that day, I took him around all my old haunts at the farm. He loved the farmhouse and all the space outside. We walked in the garden where the apple trees were in blossom, and the wood beyond, where the ground was carpeted with bluebells. It just seemed so natural to share my life with him.

Admittedly, I had some qualms when news of our engagement spread. Some friends disapproved, thinking it was too soon after Eric's death. Had I forgotten him so quickly? I couldn't explain at the time that I could never forget Eric. He had made a profound impact on my life. My ties with Eric were closely linked to God, and as I was acutely aware that God was present with me I was not likely to forget Eric. Eric himself had prepared me for this event by advising me to get married again. If Eric had not encouraged me to remarry, I wouldn't have considered it. I would have hugged the memory of him too closely to my heart. I was capable of being too wrapped up in him. From Eddy's point of view, it wasn't soon enough. He didn't want to lose me to someone else. He was aware of the many miles between us and he longed for us to be together permanently. A widowed friend of the family had things in proper perspective when she heard me fretting about wedding preparations. She said, "You have met a wonderful person, that's all that matters." Who cares about wedding preparations, was her attitude. She had known loss, struggled to bring up her large family on her own. I was having a second chance of sharing life with someone who shared my interests, which was of inestimable value.

The A.O.G. Home Missions ran an Outreach Crusade for two weeks in a seaside town in North Wales. They brought in an evangelist, erected a tent and the crowds increased almost every night. At the end of the two weeks it was decided, because the response was so good, to continue another week. During the Crusade I spent two weekends with Eddy and the team. It was interesting to observe his easy manner with everyone. All the team members had come for a working holiday and were smiling and relaxed. They held beach meetings in the afternoon and tent meetings in the evening.

A team was sent out to do follow up work in the mornings, to contact those who had attended the meetings. I accompanied Eddy and a team member; I wasn't comfortable with this approach, meeting total strangers. When we set out to knock on doors, it was quite a task to decipher people's writing, to make out their names and addresses scribbled on cards. When we got a response to our knock, some people told us they didn't understand why they had signed the cards. We told people that we were continuing the meetings during the winter, in the Badminton hall, Sunday mornings. We were a bit disheartened at the lack of interest; some of the team just shrugged and said, "Not to worry; Rome wasn't built in a day". Eventually, the Crusade ended, the big tent was dismantled, all the equipment was packed away, the team waved goodbye and we were left on our own. I wondered how we would plant a church with so little interest shown.

We didn't have much time to dwell on it for our wedding was to be held in Ireland in a few days time. In fact, I didn't expect to be in Wales at the close of the Crusade with final wedding preparations to be taken care of, but I had found out from a solicitor in Dublin that Eddy wouldn't get a marriage licence in time for the wedding because he hadn't lived in Ireland for at least a month. I was in a panic, and John suggested I go over to Wales to get married legally immediately after the Crusade finished. We could get a licence more easily in Wales than in Ireland. As soon as everything was cleared up following the Crusade, we made a dash to the Registry Office with two members of the team in tow Janet and George, to stand as witnesses, and then we rushed to Holyhead to catch the ferry to Dublin.

Two days later, Ist September 1973, we had our church wedding in the Presbyterian Church, Lower Abbey St. The service was conducted by Jim McGlade, the new pastor who had come from the North of Ireland with his wife, Vivian, to fill the vacancy left by Eric's death, in the little church in Gardiner St. Jim and Vivian had lived with me for three months prior to the wedding. Vivian had a lovely singing voice, and sang a song of consecration at the wedding. The events of the day seemed to go very fast, and before we knew it we were off on our honeymoon to Scotland.

Esther was staying with my parents at the farm. We returned for her a week later and set out once more for Wales. It was a lot of travelling and we arrived very weary at our destination after midnight. Home was a caravan parked at a farm about 14 miles outside the town. Eddy had bought a second-hand caravan during the Crusade, and a helpful suggestion was made by a nurse who came to the tent meetings that Eddy should talk to her father about moving the caravan on to his land. The arrangement was made on condition that we feed his pheasants and walk his dog, which we were happy to do.

The next morning was Sunday, and it was a rush to get to church on time but we looked forward to meeting up with some of the people we'd met on our walkabouts. Our first service was rather an anti-climax. There were three teenagers waiting for the service. Two of the girls giggled a lot and talked to each other in Welsh, Eddy had met them through the Crusade and tried now to chat with them but I think they missed the hype of the Crusade and were not interested in regular meetings. The third girl was more persistent in asking questions and had often invited us to her home during the Crusade. She was more curious about spiritual things. The two younger girls very kindly gave us a wedding present and we gave them a lift home afterwards. We were disappointed that they never came again. Soon the other girl went to University (Eddy encouraged her to join a Christian Union); and we were left with a lot of unanswered questions, especially the main one, what exactly had gone wrong?

We felt very discouraged. So much time and effort, and so much money spent on this Crusade and it all seemed wasted, except for that one genuine conversion, the young student going off to University. We tried to adjust to all this disappointment and Eddy cancelled the booking for the Badminton hall and made arrangements to hire a room in the Community Centre for a weeknight to develop acquaintance with five or six people he'd made contact with through further knocking on doors. We were very isolated unless we travelled some distance to a Sunday meeting held in Caernarfon. These meetings were the result of a similar crusade to ours; somehow there was more interest shown in that town for the meeting was well attended.

The meetings in the Community Centre ran for a time but soon faded out through lack of interest. Eddy was keen to build up contact and friendships with people through work rather than knocking on doors anymore. At work, he had great conversations with the head gardener, Wynn*, and during lunch they enjoyed playing chess together or Eddy invited him to dinner. Wynn's wife had left him and he used to find that he could talk to Eddy about his loss.

Now that it was winter the fire in the caravan smoked too

much; we sold the caravan to the farmer and moved to a farmhouse in a beautiful valley four miles from the town. The rent was six pounds per week. I found this idyllic setting a perfect refuge after all the major changes in my young life.

During the month of February, the Home Missions Secretary wanted to pay a visit to the area and check out the church plant in Caernarfon and our meeting at the Community Centre. He arranged to meet Eddy at the Centre and he stayed with us overnight; leaving early in the morning.

Eddy had been feeling unwell for some months, complaining of back pain. We put it down to the hard physical work he was involved in, doing landscape work at a caravan park to supplement our income from Home Missions. So we were astounded when, after some tests were carried out, he was told he had gout! We laughed because it sounded so absurd. We thought that only elderly rich men got that ailment when they drank too much wine! Eddy was only 22 now, and here the doctors were telling him that he should wear a back support. He went out and bought it but after a few weeks of wearing it he discarded it, commenting, "I might as well be wearing a straitjacket!"

We had made a commitment to stay with the project for a year, but with Eddy's health problems and our landlady wanting to use the house for tourists during the summer we left after nine months. Wynn tried hard to persuade Eddy to stay in the area and continue the job at the caravan park, but our minds were made up. We moved to Felixstowe, Suffolk, to live temporarily with Eddy's parents. It took us a long time to get over the experience in Wales. We felt we had failed but with the benefit of hindsight I see it as a learning experience. In one sense Eddy had satisfied himself regarding this kind of work. We felt isolated and realized in order to succeed a small team of people was necessary to share the burden. I didn't particularly feel I was gifted for this kind of project; unlike Eddy I had no training and found it extremely tough. Eddy's parents had pastored a church in Lincolnshire for fourteen years and he had supported them as a teenager. Hence, he had grown up believing he should serve God in a similar way but, in fact, he also was trying to find his niche and it was proving more difficult than he expected.

In the years that followed, it seemed God was more interested with building strong character and helping us to know exactly what was our calling and to exercise patience in waiting for the right opportunity, than helping us follow our goal of serving him in some church work. Whenever we tried a door of opportunity it was slammed firmly shut. While we waited for doors to open, Eddy worked as a shipping clerk, and with his knowledge of Swedish, that he had learned from his mother, enjoyed meeting the captains of ships that came through Felixstowe port, as he helped them through the customs procedures.

We'd been hoping for a baby for some time. Once again when I became pregnant I was sick morning and evening for many months. It was a most perplexing time; I lost sight of our goals; each day seemed to run into the next, with no real purpose. Inwardly, I battled with depression but I was unable to talk about my feelings. I felt that I was walking in a shadow land. Life had lost its colour. I felt unloved, even though rationally speaking Eddy was very caring and affectionate to me. He teased that surely I should be able to shake the sickness off, you know, mind over matter; as if I could control my mindset but I didn't know how to do this. I felt I couldn't speak of my inner battle because the people I was in contact with had comparatively easy pregnancies and loved having babies. The other problem was that I couldn't take any medication, no matter how mild, to alleviate the sickness for fear of harming the baby. It is good to know that there are now alternative remedies to overcome this sickness; and I've read some helpful advice that a mother-to-be doesn't need to feel guilty about changes in her mood. It's normal at this time to feel delicate and emotional even to feel life is out of control. But I was also dealing with the depressive nature of an anorexic and this I couldn't fathom at the time.

Naturally, there was tension living with Eddy's parents. It's always difficult to share indefinitely, even with those we love. We wanted to rent a flat in the town but when we made inquiries we found the rent was so high as the town was a popular seaside resort. Eddy's Mum tried to make things easier by turning one of the attic bedrooms into a kitchen for us to use. We had a kitchen and bedroom on the third floor, and a sitting room on the second floor. The situation greatly improved now that we had our own kitchen space.

In May '75 we had a baby daughter. I was thrilled to have another child. Two years before it looked like this would never happen again. We rejoiced in the child of our union because of our special relationship, and so we named her Joy. (As we had met so shortly after Eric's death, we were both conscious we'd been brought together in special circumstances.) Since Esther's birth was such a blur, I opted for a drug free delivery this time. I'd been told at the antenatal classes that a second baby would be born quicker that the first. The speed of Joy's delivery took my breath away. It was all over within 40 minutes of my arrival at the hospital!

Five months before Joy's birth Eddy had applied to adopt Esther. I, in effect, had to adopt Esther as well because I had married again and changed my name. Two months later we were told that a Probation Officer had been appointed by the Court to investigate the application. This meant that the Probation Officer came to visit us in our home to observe our interaction with Esther. The Officer was a single person in her thirties, very professional with an obvious love for children and a great deal of patience. We spent a comfortable hour together while Esther entertained us all with her baby talk and showing off her toys.

Three weeks following Joy's birth we presented ourselves at the Juvenile Court along with Esther. This was a big day for us, especially Eddy, who had wanted the relationship with Esther to become legal. He could now lawfully call her his daughter. When we returned home he held the two girls in his arms and hugged them tight. Our family was complete, or so we thought.

In many ways we were content, if only there was an opening for pastoral work again. Towards the end of 1975, Eddy's boss asked him if he'd move to London to start a new office and it was while we were getting settled we heard of a church vacancy in North West London. We visited the outgoing pastor, considered prayerfully the whole issue and eventually agreed to take up the pastorate the following June. In May '76, we were devastated to hear that the whole thing had fallen through for the outgoing pastor. It hit us hard because Eddy had already sent in a letter of resignation to his boss and we had given up the lease on our flat. We were bitterly disappointed and felt God was far away;

The same week we heard the bad news, we both contracted mumps! We couldn't believe that we had caught a children's disease. Eddy received some ribbing that mumps could have a bad effect on a man's sperm and lessen his chances of fathering a child. Well, Eddy wasn't thinking of fathering any more children. A baby was the last thing on our minds.

In time, we found peace again, employment (he found another job with the same firm) and a new home back in Felixstowe. Eddy was a quiet influence in the work place, always ready to give a listening ear to those in difficulty, building friendships through a game of chess or football, sometimes inviting them home to dinner.

I think we were probably too hard on ourselves, forcing an opening into what we believed our area of service should be. We gradually stopped fussing, went to a different denomination, temporarily, simply because we had no car just then and couldn't travel the 14 miles to the A.O.G. church. We attended a lovely Baptist church where the Bible teaching was so instructive. We began to relax. Some people thought we had backslidden. Christians are frequently judgmental of others when they see they're not conforming to their concept of what a Christian should do. All we needed was space to rest and enjoy our marriage without the pressure of a particular denomination's expectations upon us.

It came about very spontaneously, that we were asked to look after a youth club for 10 year olds. It was the best thing for Eddy. Here, he was himself, telling stories, playing guitar, throwing himself into the project with great energy. I found I liked this kind of work too, baking with the kids, and doing simple crafts. It was the happiest year of our marriage.

We had also got involved with a local prayer group mid week, run by a couple that attended the Anglican Church. They were very interested in the Charismatic move and they

It Happened Again

stirred our interest. They heard an Anglican minister was visiting a church in Ipswich; this man had come into a new freedom, and by simply moving with the flow and direction of God's Spirit, others were blessed when they came in contact with him.

We attended the meeting one Saturday afternoon. I thought in passing that it was quite unusual for us to go to a Church of England, especially on a Saturday afternoon. We were amazed to find the place packed to capacity; people were singing with great enthusiasm and were absorbed in the worship. At the close of his talk, the minister encouraged people to form a prayer line, with some he spent a little longer praying that they might receive the Baptism in the Holy Spirit. There was an air of expectancy such as I'd never witnessed in an Anglican church before. The old building pulsed with new life. Eddy and I were excited to see that what we had experienced in the Pentecostal churches was now spreading to the mainline churches. It had actually been taking place in different parts of England since the mid-sixties. At our next house meeting there was a great buzz of conversation about what took place. It encouraged people to look for greater blessing in the Spirit, and to look for healing both physical and emotional.

Eddy and I also got involved in a singing group with people we had come to know through our connections in the Baptist church. We formed a small group, about seven of us, and practised new songs that had come in with the recent tide of the Charismatic renewal. We had two guitarists for backing, of which Eddy was one. After we sang a medley of songs one of the group shared a short meditation. We were invited to a number of different churches. We were excited and enthusiastic at the possibilities under God's leading. For a time, it seemed to take off but then, sadly, one member of the group ran into personal difficulties. His struggle shook us all and shortly after, the group broke up.

During that period, we learned a song that was making a statement about the change that God makes in a person's life; that it was real without a doubt. Eddy used to love strumming away on his guitar alone, and this was one of his favourite songs. One day, for the fun of it, he got the tape recorder out, and recorded himself making weird and wonderful chords, and then finished up with this song. I teased him that he fancied himself a star. Later, I was so thankful to have the recording in my possession. Despite the breaking up of the group, it didn't shatter Eddy's faith, quite the contrary. It was a time of strengthening his faith and I believe that it was the same for most of the others involved in the group. Our hearts grieved for our friend who withdrew from a loving church environment.

In the Spring of '78, Eddy began to speak much of Ireland. I was most surprised, thinking I'd left it for good. When I'd married Eddy, I believed it meant leaving family, friends and country. Now, because Eddy was keen to move, I was excited about returning to my homeland. I remembered God's promise for Ireland and I was eager to see how things were progressing. Even before I left Dublin in '73, there were interesting changes taking place, especially in Eustace St. (Dublin) where great numbers of people, many Catholic, were finding a new dimension in God. We had heard from John and Joy, that the Charismatic Renewal had touched many people, particularly those who had left the mainstream churches.

On our return home, we found a new openness to God's Holy Spirit. There were mixed feelings and opinions on the

Charismatic Renewal, but I think there were some outstanding results. Present day understanding shows that the fears expressed at the time were unfounded. It opened up the whole country; people's thinking changed about religion and there can now be found groups of spirit-filled Christians in every major town. In Dublin alone, there are more than 30 new churches.

Back then in '78 we were interested in buying a house in the country on an acre of land to make it a welcome retreat for our city friends especially those involved in church work and experiencing stress. If we could not be in this kind of work, ourselves, we wanted to help those who were involved. We had read in The Irish Post that industry and exports were booming in Ireland, and most of all that house prices were so attractive particularly around Westmeath. One house we read about was too good to miss, you wouldn't see a detached house like that with an acre of land for miles around Felixstowe at the low price of ten thousand pounds! We aimed to be self-sufficient, to live off the land as much as possible, by growing our own vegetables and keeping chickens. Who knows, when things were established we might even buy a few cattle from my Dad? Anything was possible.

When Eddy had worked as a gardener in North Wales, he had gained experience in growing tomatoes in a glasshouse. He had already done research in the local library on how to grow mushrooms and had some practise in the tiny shed at the bottom of our garden. He asked Dad for his copies of the Farmer's Journal to gain more ideas to utilise the land to best advantage. He even considered buying more land later to open a caravan park. There were a few lakes in the vicinity, and the tourists were visiting the beauty spots. There was great potential. His mind was bubbling with ideas and he spent his evenings jotting them down and planning.

We made a decision to cash a life insurance policy to finance our move to Ireland. We thought a few months would make little difference; we could so easily take another policy out once we got settled. How wrong we were!

Eddy went over to Ireland first to find a job, he took Joy with him to stay with my Mum while I prepared for a music exam and Esther finished off the school term. This was quite an adventure for a three year old and for days beforehand Joy talked of nothing else but travelling on a ship to see Gran and Granddad in Ireland. Eddy loaded up the old Corsair with his gear, Esther's ginger cat, Tuppence, who was sedated to keep him quiet during the journey and my canary, Woodhouse, was in his cage with an old curtain thrown over so he wouldn't be alarmed; and little Joy securely buckled in the front seat. I received a letter a few days later to tell me that the journey was unusually quiet, what with a drugged cat, a canary who couldn't sing and a little girl who had tummy-ache. Poor Joy got sick and Eddy had to stop at a service station to wash her, and change her clothes. Once they got on the boat Joy came to life and they explored the decks. At the farm, Joy watched eagerly the calves being fed and the cows brought in for milking. It was all so new to her.

One evening Eddy attended a prayer meeting in John and Joy's home. John had a vision of the house we intended to buy. At this point Eddy hadn't described the house in detail to John. He was amazed at John's accurate description like the estate agent's flyer, a double-fronted house, two-storey, the position of the house on the fork of the road. Eddy was excited at God revealing this; there must be some good reason for it. Our future would be secure. He wasn't so sure when John continued recounting his vision. He saw dark clouds over the house. "This is the house the Lord has for you", he told Eddy, "but you may question whether you've made the right move." It was with mixed feelings that Eddy shared this vision with me when he returned to England to help me pack up our belongings.

We moved in three months later, reassured that it was the right place, but puzzled by the additional words where we might question if we'd done the right thing. What could possibly go wrong?

We attended the local church sometimes on Sunday mornings; and in the evenings we went to Mullingar to a house meeting looking for a little more spiritual input. Dave and Betty McKeag, an American couple, received us warmly and were very supportive during this transition period.

Eddy got a job lorry driving, often driving long distances. He had tried a few jobs such as landscape gardening, joinery, and now lorry driving collecting offal. The down side of this job meant he came home smelling like a tip, but it paid better than the other jobs, and there was a possibility he might get a job with a grain merchant in a few month's time.

With Eddy away from early morning I was at a disadvantage not being able to drive. I felt cut off out in the middle of the countryside. Everything had been so convenient in Felixstowe. I had to rely on a friend giving Esther a lift to school. The sooner I learned to drive the better. But I was beginning to feel so lethargic and unwell. How could I have lost my enthusiasm for the country so soon?

When I started having bouts of morning sickness you could have knocked me down with a feather I was that shocked. I liked the English idea of a typical family with two children, that's the way we planned it. This was a surprise baby that cut across my plans. Eddy was excited about it. He said, "Well, the mumps didn't make me sterile. Perhaps it will be a boy this time." We discussed names, Eddy suggested calling him Nathaniel, as we wanted to use Eric's middle name and James, his middle name. I agreed but pointed out that it could easily be another girl. It was better to have a name planned.

"Call her Helen." Eddy replied.

"That's very flattering to name her after me, but think of the mix up when one of us would be called."

We consulted a book of names to find another form of 'Helen'. Amongst the alternative names we noticed the name Eleanor and decided this would be our choice.

At this point everything seemed to go wrong for me, with Eddy away so much, any renovating in the house had to wait. I thought everything looked grey and dull. It wasn't just the state of the house, the downside of pregnancy had hit again. I didn't seem to have any resources to maintain my equilibrium. Added to this, there were mice in the house; the kids couldn't play freely in the field because the septic tank was not safe. I was feeling sick most of the time, I bottled up my real feelings. We were out driving one Saturday looking for a furniture shop when I dared to voice how I really felt.

"You know, I feel absolutely nothing inside. Nothing excites me, nothing moves me."

There was silence. Eddy looked at me, astonished. Where did that come from? I, too, was astonished. In fact, I was appalled at such an admission, even frightened. I promised myself I'd never speak like that again. Nothing more was said of the incident. But things in the house remained higgledy-piggledy, and there were disturbing things pushing to the surface within me, so we decided to ask John and Joy if we could visit.

I wanted to try to communicate, and knew that John and Joy were being led in a ministry of inner healing. We visited for a weekend but somehow I was quite ill on the Saturday evening and was unable to have that important talk.

After the long months of sickness had passed, I got used to the idea of another child and looked forward to the birth in May.

One winter evening, Eddy arrived home about 7p.m. and after changing his clothes sat eating his dinner, relating the events of his day. The children were in bed. I relaxed in an armchair by the kitchen range. Then Eddy spoke of how he feared death, but after a long struggle, God had comforted him and taken away the fear. I looked closely at Eddy. I had lived with him for five years and had never heard him talk of this fear. I was growing uncomfortable with the turn in conversation. He was silent for a while. I sensed there was more to come.

"Helen, what if I died? What would you do?"

I stared long at him before replying:

"What would I do? What do you think I'd do? I'd go mad." I was amazed we were talking this way. If I could have made an exit at this point I would have gladly done so. Everything within me was objecting to this intrusive conversation. I told him:

"I don't really want to talk about it, it just couldn't happen again." I spoke with emphasis.

"But what if it did happen," he said quietly. It felt as if something, very gently but at the same time very firmly, was compelling me to face this conversation and I couldn't turn and run away.

I found myself stuttering with a kind of helplessness. "Eddy, will you stop this.... perhaps ...it could...happen. But I sure hope it doesn't... surely...surely God wouldn't let it happen a second time?"

I paused a moment and then finished with these words:

"I want to live a long and happy life with you, then I'd like to die before you do. I think that's a reasonable desire, considering everything that's happened, don't you?"

He nodded in agreement and dropped the subject. Because of the way things turned out, it would seem that I was being prepared. I think that Eddy wanted me to think about it should he be taken, especially as this inner work had taken place in his heart regarding his outlook on death. Perhaps it was in God's plan to dispel his fears of death before that final journey.

We celebrated Christmas with my parents and brother, Isaac, that year although we were first intending to spend it in our own home. On Christmas Eve we had an emergency in our house, with a severe frost in the night the water froze in the toilet bowl and the bowl was cracked! So we drove to my parent's farm only thirty miles away. The highlight of the unexpected holiday for the children was the heavy snowfall, and the way Eddy built a snowman for them almost in the twinkling of an eye. His method was new to me, (I was used to packing handfuls of snow together which was a long and tedious job) he just started rolling a ball around the front lawn and it just grew and grew. And before we knew it there was a massive body planted in the middle of the lawn and Eddy was busy rolling a smaller ball for his head. The girls were naturally all excited and ran quickly to the house to get pieces of coal for his eyes, a carrot for his nose, and one of Grandad's hats decorated with a pheasant's feather to cover his head. Afterwards we warmed up in Gran's cosy kitchen sampling her Christmas baking.

On an icy cold morning in January 1979, I sat with the children at our kitchen table. We were warm and cosy with the heat from the range. Esther and Joy were absorbed in drawing and colouring pictures, while I replaced some buttons on a cardigan. I was getting ready for our weekend away in Dublin with John and Joy. I was hoping to discuss with them some pressing questions.

It was about 10.30a.m on a Saturday morning, we were eagerly awaiting Eddy's coming home from work. He had started out about 5.30a.m., to go to Castleblayney, Co. Monaghan. He hoped to make the return journey in about four and a half hours. Suddenly, our peace was disturbed by a knock on the kitchen window. I looked up to find our minister and my neighbour, Rose*, waving to us to open the front door. I hadn't heard them knock on it. As I ran to open the door, I wondered why they had come together? Looking at their faces while they greeted me, I knew, instinctively, that there was something wrong, so I sent the children upstairs.

Rose urged me to sit down but I couldn't sit with the uneasy feeling growing within me. The minister told me that Eddy had died in an accident at work. I stared at him in disbelief.

"But... this happened before. How could it happen again?" It was uncanny.

Rose pulled a chair close to me. She had miscarried when she suffered a shock and she was afraid the same would happen to me. I couldn't sit still. Someone was crying. It was my mother entering the kitchen, and Dad was distracted by her emotion suggesting she sit down and have a cup of tea. He wasn't comfortable with a show of emotion, and neither was I. It galvanised me into action. The children. What about the children? They were still up in their bedroom and they would have seen their Granny and Grandad come and wonder what was going on. I knew I had to get to them before anyone frightened them with crying and talk of accidents.

More to the point, it dawned on me that they were suddenly bereft of a father's love and protection. All this flashed through my mind as I dashed upstairs. I may have been five months pregnant, but I had no thought for myself. All my instincts cried out for my two fatherless children. I opened the bedroom door and found them playing quietly with some toys on their beds. They looked so innocent and helpless, and I was about to shatter their world. I braced myself and sat down on Joy's bunk. I explained, briefly, that their Daddy was not coming home, he was now in Heaven with Jesus. There was no question in my mind on that score, and I made sure that they knew where their father was. It would be the one certainty in the midst of many uncertainties.

"God will take care of us. Somehow. It all seems so strange, but somehow God will help us." I told them. It was something like a prayer. Esther asked a question or two, but I can't remember what she said. They were very subdued as they sensed the misfortune that had occurred. For Esther it was a second time to lose a parent. She and Eddy had got on so well together, he had never made any difference between his adopted child and his blood child. He had loved her as his own.

Now that my parents were with us and all of us were trying to grasp the situation, the minister suggested we phone Eddy's parents. As we had no phone, Rev. Flynn took me to the rectory to make the call. I dreaded telling Eddy's mother, he was her only child and my heart shrank from breaking the news to her. She always cried so easily, she had no hang-ups with her emotions, how would I handle it? I shrank from showing any expression of grief. She came on the line greeting me warmly. As I started to tell her the news, my voice choked up. I had not cried for myself, but I cried brokenly for her. To my surprise, my Mum-in-law did not cry, she was concerned for me.

When I arrived back home, neighbours started to call. I hardly knew them; we were living in the area such a short time. It was like deja vu; only for me it wasn't an illusion. It had happened again! I could hardly believe that I had lost a husband again within a few short years. Almost the same events were happening; someone coming to tell me the bad news; a trip to the hospital mortuary; a funeral to arrange; a baby soon to be born. The only difference this time was that I lost my home as well, for we had not had time to arrange a mortgage protection. My world had caved in again, but even while I struggled to grasp the facts, something rose up within me that spurred me into action. I was determined to provide for, and protect my children at all costs. Yes, it was a mother's instinctive reaction, but there was also an added quality, the voice of faith told me, it insisted; that I would find a way to fend for my children, despite this unmerciful blow.

My mother was anxious to get me to the doctor. He might prescribe sleeping tablets. I was relieved when we found he was out on a call, I didn't want sleeping tablets. All I wanted was to return to the farm, my childhood home. I did not care to stay another moment in the house in Westmeath. With Eddy gone I had lost all interest in it. About an hour after we got to the farm, the news flashed across the television screen about Eddy's accident. It had occurred in a butcher's yard in Castleblayney. There were no witnesses at the scene of the accident. Eddy had parked the lorry on a slope, which was very icy, and during the procedure of swinging a full skip onto his lorry, the lorry had slipped to the side on the icy surface and pinned Eddy up against a refrigerator container. Death was believed to be instantaneous. Were they really talking about Eddy? My husband? At that moment it seemed so strange, so unreal. I couldn't take in the details. If only I could see Eddy's body for myself. Because I hadn't as yet seen Eddy's body, part of me couldn't accept fully that he was dead. I expected to see him come through the door any moment. This feeling remained until, two days later; my father and brother took me to the hospital mortuary. As soon as I saw Eddy's still form I knew he was gone.

The words pronounced in most funerals are found in the story of Lazarus, "I am the Resurrection and the Life. He who believes in me will live, even though he dies...."[1] Jesus spoke these words to Martha concerning her brother, Lazarus. For Lazarus it was a physical resurrection. For Eddy, now, he had passed from one dimension into another. Jesus had reassured him there was life beyond the grave and that he was not to fear the transition, whenever that event took place. On the 27th January 1979 at the age of 27, Eddy crossed over into his new life.

Eddy's body was moved from the hospital mortuary to my parents' church in Moynalty where a short service was held. Dave McKeag shared about his ties with Eddy and myself and spoke of his appreciation to Eddy in supporting him and his wife in their outreach work in Mullingar. It was a spontaneous tribute, it was not planned and I think we were all surprised that he stood up to speak. I was so grateful for his kind words that day.

Eddy's body remained in the church a few days until his parents arrived from England. On the morning of the funeral we travelled to the A.O.G. church (that used to be based in Gardiner St. but was now located in an old Methodist Church in

Dolphins Barn, Dublin.) Jim McGlade waited to take the service. Eddy and I were the first couple whose marriage he officiated over, now Eddy was the first person whose funeral he led. As I approached the door of the church, our friend, Bob McAlister, sympathised with me and shared the verse "You do not realize now what I am doing, but later you will understand."[2] This verse had been the text used at Eric's funeral. I thought it was significant that it should be pointed out to me again. I can't remember much about the service or the committal. I was told later that the gravediggers seemed pressed for time and rather rushed the prayers around the grave. It didn't trouble me, for once again I felt cushioned and protected, the same as at Eric's funeral. It seemed I was insulated from disturbance of any kind.

Eddy's life made a great impression on many, especially one friend who decided to go to Bible College with the intention of entering the ministry. His former boss in the Shipping Company sent a tribute to the family. He mentioned that Eddy was a special kind of person with a disarming honesty and cheerful disposition. He remembered Eddy's ability for getting into scrapes and then later admitting everything. This was unusual in a business where everyone relies on talking his or her way out of scrapes. He thought the commercial world was not the place for Eddy; somehow "he was above the petty dishonesties which flavours modern business." He assured us we were in his thoughts and prayers; and while it was a very distressing time we should remember that Eddy was "an exceptional person as a son, husband and for the children – father- even though it was for so short a time."

I would like to include the following account entitled "My

Dad" which Esther wrote for school homework. It was written about two years after Eddy died, she wrote it as if he was still alive.

"My Dad is nice and loving, he is kind and does what's right. He's a lorry driver and I often go with him at the weekends in the lorry. When I went with him he always bought me something from the shops. Sometimes I would take a pencil and paper and write down the numbers of the cars. He said he would buy me a book to write about cars. He has a stamp book and I often read it."

For anyone bereaved, they go through a stage of questioning. Why did it happen? Surely it seems so senseless and cruel. It has been voiced in some Christian circles that we shouldn't question the Almighty. What has happened is the will of God, so we should accept it. I don't think it is harmful to question so long as it is constructive and uplifting. I found that through my questions, through some points that friends made in their letters and thoughts gained from reading certain books over a number of years all helped me through this stage.

To begin with, a former pastor wrote, touching on the way God tests his people. I have mentioned Job in a previous chapter. Job was severely tested; he lost all his children; his stock; and his health. It was a wonder Job hadn't been driven mad. As he sat amongst the ashes of his property he wished he'd never been born. This was a natural reaction in the circumstances. He was speaking out of the depths of great sorrow and anguish. I had suffered two losses and was groping for answers. What purpose could there possibly be in this? I was discovering that God tests his people to know the intentions of their heart, to see if they are willing to follow his commands or not.[3]

The example of Job was showing me that I could be certain that God had a gracious design in testing my faith. He would not destroy what is precious and worthwhile in the refining process, only what is useless.[4] It raised another question. Why does God allow suffering and loss if He is such a loving God? From my understanding of Job, he does not receive an answer to his question, but he comes to recognise the sovereignty of God over all He has made. He learned to submit to the will of God. In the furnace of affliction and loss I was learning to see things from God's perspective. I don't know how it happens, but when we go through a major test we just don't come out the same as we went in. We either come out bitter and resentful, or we see what is most important. Our priorities are different. The righteous are tested by divine love, this makes all the difference, because they are under God's protection and care.

How much can one person bear? Sandy Thompson came to speak at one of our Easter meetings, 1979. He related to me a vision he had about this point concerning me. He explained about the Plimsoll line, on the hull of a ship. If a ship is overloaded, it is likely to be unstable. If God overloaded me with burdens I couldn't bear, the "ship" of my life would be wrecked. Sandy emphasized the point: God would not test me more than I was able to bear. My load would not exceed the 'PLIMSOLL LINE'

All these things shaped my thinking in the face of severe testing. In the days following the funeral, I questioned, a lot, why we ever moved to Westmeath and tried to buy that house. I recalled the vision John had of the dark clouds over the house and how he had said that we would question the move? Yet, it prepared us for the hard blow. The dark clouds were probably a warning that something was going to happen. We could look back on these things (e.g. John's vision, Eddy speaking about death), and say God was there. In a strange way that was reassuring.

In 1981, our friend, Bill Turner, who has a pastoral and prophetic ministry shared a vision with me. He saw me receive two blows over the head with a sledgehammer, the blows drove me into the ground almost to the knees but my back remained straight. The point about my back not buckling was impressed so much on him that he drew a rough picture of his vision for me to keep. I was still standing despite two tragic events.

FOUR

Single Parent

JOHN AND JOY invited me to stay with them until I found a place to live. Mum and Dad said we could stay longer at the farm, but I knew that if I was to remain independent I must go to the city where there was a lot more opportunity to achieve my goal at that time. John and my mother helped me to pack up my belongings in Westmeath while Joy took care of the children. As I travelled to the house for the last time, the thought entered my mind that one day I would write my story to help others in similar circumstances. I hid this thought in my heart for future consideration.

Back in Dublin, Bob McAlister, a voluntary and religious worker, told us to pile our boxes high in the bedroom I shared with my two girls in John and Joy's house so that the representative from the Housing Department would see how urgently we needed a place. When the representative came and saw our circumstances, we were assured that they would try everything possible to get us a place of our own soon. John and Joy were a tremendous support to us during these uncertain days. John was a father figure to the girls helping somewhat to alleviate the great gap in their lives.

My baby was born in the early hours of 10th May, a week

before the due date. I had another little girl. It was all very quiet and subdued. Back then, the Coombe Hospital didn't allow a relative to sit with the expectant mother, if a husband were unable to be present. It would have been helpful while I was in the pre-labour ward not necessarily during the birth. The pains had died down on arriving at the hospital, and I lay for more than an hour drifting in and out of sleep. Then things started to happen and I was moved into the labour ward, it was towards the end that the pain increased and I was offered some gas. It helped me over the worst part. I could have done with my mother's comforting presence, when reaction set in following the birth. A nurse had taken the baby away already to be washed and put in the nursery. I'd hardly got a look at her. It was while I waited for a doctor to give me stitches, that I felt so cold I began to tremble uncontrollably. The nurses were busy in another part of the room and I felt bereft. I didn't want to interrupt them and ask for an extra blanket. I felt close to emotional break down, and was fighting hard to hold myself together.

The next morning I held my 'surprise' baby in my arms. Now that she was born, it didn't matter that she had interrupted my life, neither did it matter that she wasn't a boy. I was bonding with this sweet, brown-eyed baby. She had lots of dark hair and she was smaller in weight than my other girls. She was perfect in every way.

At least to me she was perfect. But two days later, one of the doctors scheduled tests to examine the baby. These tests are usually a matter of routine; I had seen them carried out on my other children. This time the doctor's attitude bothered me. My heart was beating fast as I watched him check Eleanor's head, and limbs. Then he checked her head again and again, frowning a lot and whispering to the nurse. I asked the doctor what he was looking for, but he avoided my questions. I grew frightened, but thought to myself:

"I'm not going to get all worked up over this." I tried to pray quietly. The examination lengthened out, the whispering continued, they were saying something about a further test, until finally the doctor ruled that out. He was satisfied that the baby was all right. He covered her with the blanket, smiled and left the ward.

I lay back against the pillows, exhausted. Why did he put me through that ordeal? Why couldn't he have examined her in the nursery, and only tell me if there was something really wrong? Didn't he know that I had gone through enough already; I had faced the birth without the support of my husband. I felt badly shaken and longed to talk to Eddy. I felt my control slipping, and so fought hard to push the thoughts away. Gradually, the distress eased and I lifted Eleanor from the cot for her next feed. Inwardly, I thanked God that there was nothing wrong with her. She was healthy, that was all that mattered. I had to content myself with telling Mum and Joy about the episode later on, but it was a brief version with none of the feelings that had agitated me in the morning. I couldn't describe to them how alarmed and distraught I had really felt, or I would have gone to pieces.

Joy Gray came to collect us from the hospital, with Leslie, Esther and Joy. The children admired the newcomer in her cosy baby nest. Back at the house Joy made a lovely meal, she tried to make everything as comfortable as possible, but it wasn't our house and there was a big gap. Someone was missing from that homecoming and there was a subdued atmosphere. Suddenly, Esther began to cry, then Joy sobbed and I started too, struggling to keep some measure of control. I rose from the table and took refuge upstairs. I couldn't cope with the children's emotion. I was afraid to lose control. It was necessary to check my feelings; the alternative would be like slipping into a darkness I couldn't face. Despite all this, Eleanor's birth united a grieving family in hope. Her coming gave us something to live for in the face of heart wrenching loss.

It was that same evening I met David and Fiona Burke. They came to the Monday night meeting held weekly in John and Joy's house. They came upstairs to admire the new baby. David and Fiona were just married the month before, and they talked a little about their honeymoon trip. I expected to make friends with some widow at the Widow's Association I attended, but their talk of feelings about their husbands made me feel uncomfortable at that time, so I left the Association. I wasn't ready to sort out my feelings. It was alien to me. So it was a tremendous support to find a friend in Fiona; whose hunger and longing for God matched my own hunger and our friendship grew rapidly. Over the years we got involved in Sunday school together and Worship ministry. These activities proved to be great growing points. David was a tremendous support he, too, became another father figure in the children's lives. His sense of humour livened up many an occasion when he came to a meal or to do repairs.

In July, I obtained a Maisonette from the Corporation. We had waited just five months for a placement. It was a far cry from the open spaces of the countryside, but it was ours to call home. I moved in with plans to teach music once again. I bought a reconditioned piano for two hundred pounds. It had a highly polished mahogany veneer which looked very impressive. When I was discussing delivery with the proprietor and told him the piano was to be delivered to an upstairs flat, he wasn't very keen to undertake the job. I told him it was very important I have a piano; there must be a way to get it upstairs. He thought about it awhile and decided to take the front part off, the actual keyboard, so the men could grip the main bulk of the piano and carry it upstairs safely. The job was carried out with only minor damage to the carpet on the stairs.

I discovered that God has a special place in his heart for the widow and orphans, there are some very tender verses on the subject; "A Father to the fatherless, a defender of widows". "The Lord...sustains the fatherless and the widow". "You hear, O Lord, the desire of the afflicted; You encourage them, and you listen to their cry, defending the fatherless and the oppressed..."[1] I felt that we were under the wings of His protection, that He would defend us in our brokenness.

The flat was in need of decorating and in the long winter evenings some of our church friends came and helped to put up Winnie the Pooh wallpaper in the bathroom, and paint our kitchen that was so small you couldn't swing a cat! For us having recently moved to the city it was a tremendous support to be linked up to a big church family.

My parents did not share my views or enthusiasm for the church I had chosen up to this point, but they were very troubled over Eddy's death. They missed his light-hearted conversations when we spent weekends on the farm. They liked his knack of finding jobs to do without being asked. They were, naturally, concerned for my welfare and did everything possible for the children and me. In my contact with John and Joy, Mum and Dad were drawn into their circle of friends and meetings. This added a new dimension to their lives. Gradually they opened up their hearts to the Lord in a way they had not done before, even though they were committed churchgoers. Dad, especially, was challenged by a vision one person had for him where he was only allowing Jesus to enter 'by the back door' to his life. He allowed the Lord to come in more on that occasion and it softened him somewhat. Yet he still had difficulty to be open after this because of past hurts in his life.

For about three years I worked hard to establish a routine and lifestyle that would benefit my children. I would talk very matter-of-fact if anyone touched on the tragedy, but I would not reveal my true feelings. I had locked my feelings firmly away; I could not speak of the utter devastation I felt inwardly. It went too deep to try to communicate. Left alone, all my insecurities came to the surface. These three children were dependent on me. What sort of example was I to them? The things that most women long for – work fulfilment, falling in love, marriage, children - these had all come to me so quickly in my young life. I didn't expect to be married and have children so young. (Regarding work, my decision to teach piano seemed promising at first; now, I wasn't so sure.) The romance, fun and companionship were gone, and I was left with the children, and time to reflect. People would say to me, "But you have the children." I know they meant well, and yes, I loved my children very much, and they kept me focused, but people didn't know how much those words bothered me. I had lost my partner, my companion, my lover, and my helpmate whom I had looked forward to sharing the responsibilities of these little ones. I thought we would face it together. But I never gave voice to these feelings.

To add to my sense of loss was the disappointment that I had never gained the Diploma in music. I felt a failure; I had not reached my own expectations or those of my family. I felt I wasn't adequately qualified to teach, yet officials in the Royal Irish

Academy of Music never made any queries about qualifications when I entered pupils for examinations. Several pupils passed with excellent results. I set about improving my achievements by attending the Academy for regular lessons. I doubted my ability from an early age, and constantly compared myself to others.

At this time, I did not know how to bring my failure to God, therefore my efforts to cope got in the way. Soon, I was a driven person, for I felt I was failing in every area. At one stage I was taking lessons in driving, sewing, music, anything to quieten the accusing voice that drummed within my head. Things were out of perspective and I drove myself on.

I tried to be brave and get on with my life, not to bother anyone. But I was overloading my system, some days I would arrive home from the Academy totally exhausted. I would slump in a chair unable to prepare tea for the children. I was, secretly, alarmed with the upsurge of the eating disorder that had started in my teens. I thought for a while it was fairly much under control, but I would go on binges frequently, then starve for a couple of days.

Inwardly, I knew I wasn't coping well, which only increased my erratic eating habits. Without the presence of another adult, the deception continued. For months I pressed on, then with my cycle disturbed I attended the Hospital for treatment. There were no questions asked of any importance as to the root cause of my problem, the nurse said that I was too thin for my build and asked if I was eating enough, and because I had convinced myself that I was eating enough I said, yes. She handed me a prescription for medicine, which eventually restored my cycle, but the side effects left me depressed. I grew increasingly irritable with the children and my workload.

Eleanor's birth, coming as it did, in the midst of a second

bereavement, touched a cord deep within me. I could not as easily shut up the fountain of my emotions. A new softening, very gradual at first, was taking place. It affected most noticeably my reactions to Esther and Joy when they misbehaved. I was very strict with them before the tragedy, rapping out commands just as they had been rapped out to me as a child. How often do you hear it said, "I'm not going to act with my kids like my parents did with me." Yet time and again we do the same things because of the role model we had in childhood.

There was a lot of anger in me and I couldn't understand why. It would erupt every so often when the kids pressed certain switches that set me off. (Just like my father had erupted with us.) I would be deeply ashamed and apologise to them and hope it would never happen again. I would work hard to contain it, weeks would go by until the next time they pressed a button and I was off again. In my childhood, I had never been given any guidelines for handling anger. I never knew, while growing up, that my anger was showing up some problem that needed to be addressed. It was always considered a negative thing, something to be avoided at all costs. Because I was given to angry outbursts as a child, I was labelled as the one with the bad temper. And what hurt more was the way I was reminded that I was like some relative who had a rotten temper. All it did was to pile shame on my head. Nobody ever sat me down to ask me why I was so angry.

For a long while Esther and Joy said that I spoiled Eleanor. I think now, that they were right, but I hope they can understand that she was born during a second period of great loss that gradually brought about a major change in me. Although it was a slow process, they, too, reaped the benefits of that softening in me.

These angry outbursts and the need in me to drive myself, was now getting my attention but I still did not know how to put it right. As much as I wanted to prove myself and seek acceptance from those I loved, I had to listen to my body's needs. I was wearing myself out; something had to give. I sobbed out my distress to Fiona, it was my immediate distress of an impossible workload, not any deeper emotions. I didn't realise how deep my emotions were buried. But it was the beginning of a series of inner healings. There was a shortage of Christian counsellors at that time, and so I was directed into healing in a gentle way, to begin with, that appealed to me very much. Fiona handed me a praise tape that day that lifted me out of my distress. I began to listen to worship tapes, learning the value of personal praise. Slowly, I was finding the path to joy in worship that I had first witnessed with Eric.

However it was a breakdown of sorts; I was finding it hard to cope. I was suffering from depression and fatigue but I didn't vocalize that I was depressed. My neighbour, Rita, was a tremendous help in taking Eleanor for a few hours while Esther and Joy were at school. I had taken to my bed, and there I would sometimes listen to these tapes and they cheered me up.

I gave up the lessons at the Academy because the teachers were demanding piano practice seven days a week and extra classes, which I could not fulfil as a busy mother. They were insisting that I repeat Grade 8, which I had already passed, believing it would prepare me better for the Diploma examination. My goal of achieving the Diploma seemed years away. It had been some years since I'd prepared for an exam, and I think my teacher believed, by repeating grade eight, it would sharpen my reactions in the exam room. In later years, I saw the wisdom in this but, at the time, things were not happening fast enough for me. I thought having done it once and passed, there was no need to do it again. I never dealt with the reality that I had only barely passed.

There were so many regulations that it just seemed a repeat of all the sweat and frustration of my last year at school. Working, striving for an examination every year, feeling sick with nerves, and trembling with fear at the thought of, once again, facing a dour examiner; I was weary of the whole thing.

There was one positive aspect from my time spent at the Academy. My piano teacher, also a widow with three children; wanted to help me in my efforts to teach. She knew about my pupils coming each week. She encouraged me to buy the current books for the early grades and bring them to my class; she then showed me how to teach those pieces to my pupils.

For some years, I concentrated on activities that would benefit my children, that kept me in touch with their interests, such as taking charge of a Good News Club backed by Child Evangelism Fellowship, and I attended the monthly training classes. I helped with Sunday School, enjoying the challenges of worship and weekly lessons with the children, and planning Christmas plays. The girls found great pleasure in swimming and Girl Guides. Another interest I enjoyed, occasionally, with the children was attending music events in the National Concert Hall.

I introduced my own children to the piano while covering the first tutor book, and then sent them to another piano teacher to avoid tension building up between us. It had started in Esther when I entered her for her first piano examination; she ended up in the hospital with pains in her abdomen. We thought it was appendicitis, but following the doctor's examination, the nurse asked me if Esther was anxious about anything. It came out that she was worrying about the exam, and I blamed myself for creating tension. Esther still sat for the exam and passed with honours.

Then I was beset with thoughts about failing the Diploma, and felt driven to attend classes once again. I chose a teacher who gave lessons in her own home. I wanted to keep away from the pressure I had felt in the Academy. This time I found there was more variety in the set pieces, because I had been used to a limited range before which usually included some heavy classical pieces by Bach that sounded so mournful that I was bored with them. For a time I forgot about the exam and all the physical and emotional effects that went with it, and actually learned to appreciate the music, even some of Bach's Preludes and Fugues! That was the best time.

I took on needless pressure when I looked at how long it was taking me to reach my goal and the apprehension that assailed me when I thought of the examination room. In a way, I was programmed to think in this manner and I couldn't keep up the standard or continue the lessons. When I got caught up with planning for the exam there seemed so much restriction and negativity that it stifled my natural inclination and enjoyment. It would have been better if I had stuck to my inner feeling and said 'no' to grade eight the first time and learned for pleasure. It suited my disposition better. But pressure to achieve a certificate had been strong. By this time I felt I couldn't keep up with this punishing schedule anymore, but I could still be shaken by the opinions of others. The worry that I wasn't qualified adequately haunted me. All this was linked to the fear of man, which ruled me at this time, but I couldn't separate myself from it.

From where did all the high expectations spring? It all started when I sought my Granny's company to hear stories of her childhood, and of my father's childhood and his siblings. But I didn't hear much praise for my father, Granny had an inordinate pride in two of her children, a son and a daughter who excelled at school and went on to higher education. The son became a clergyman and the daughter became a schoolteacher. They were constantly being upheld to me as models of achievement. This is how I took my Granny's words about her children; it is not necessarily the true picture. I loved and admired this aunt and my goal was to become a school - teacher, first of all, but when I struggled with Maths I abandoned that idea. I decided I wanted to be a music teacher. I longed for my grandmother's approval, as much as my father's and set about to win that approval.

In my early years of learning the piano, I passed my exams with flying colours achieving first class honours. As I climbed the grades I came out with second-class honours. To me, it just wasn't good enough, even though the marks were well up in the 80's, and I drove myself to improve. It was the words 'second honours' that made it sound less than the best. (Nowadays, they've scrapped first and second honours and laid out the marking system differently.) My pleasure in music was no longer a pleasure, it became my private hell, the examination room was, literally, a battleground. I was caught up in my dream of obtaining a diploma and becoming a teacher partly for the wrong reasons. I pinned my hopes for approval on my achieving; I wanted my family to be proud of me. Because of this, the reality didn't penetrate my consciousness, that I drove myself too hard, I couldn't relax, I had to do well therefore I set myself up for failure.

My goal continued moving from grade to grade and making a trip once a year for the examination to the Royal Irish Academy in Dublin. Once I had achieved grade five within six months, instead of a year, I wanted to sit grade six as soon as possible. But my plans backfired when my teacher missed the entry date for the exam. I was bitterly disappointed and soon after I went on a severe diet, as I mention later. It was at this point that I left school and went to work in Dublin.

I was sick of the pressure at this stage and all I wanted was to learn music for pleasure. Through a girl at work I found a music teacher who taught in Ormond Quay. I attended classes twice a week and enjoyed freedom from exams for a whole year. Two months into my second year, I was learning "To the Spring" by Grieg. I liked the Norwegian's expression of the season; his music was melodious and light-hearted, but I doubted that I was capturing the feeling in my playing. I tended to be a bit heavy handed, and thought my tension detracted from the music. My teacher never mentioned these things. She announced that this piece was one of three pieces set for the Advanced Senior examination with the London College of Music. (I was told this was the equivalent of Grade 8.) I was flabbergasted. Did she think that I was good enough? Yes. But I would be jumping two grades. She told me I was capable; she had planned all this carefully, increasing my repertoire and ability, unknown to me, over the past year.

The following June 1971, I took the exam and was dismayed to find the result was only a pass, not even second honours. Outwardly, I pinned a smile on my face when people asked me the results. At least, I had passed it, but inside, I was deeply disappointed. The teacher had no regrets. Of course, it would have been nicer to get higher marks, she said, but better luck next time. She surprised me further by showing me pieces for the next examination, which was for the cap and gown, as she put it. My mind struggled to take in this information. Did she mean she was entering me for the diploma exam? She nodded. Something about all this didn't add up, the diploma was a tough exam. Her currant diploma students seemed far more advanced than me; but I didn't know how to articulate my concern. Her words made me feel that I would achieve my goal quicker than I had anticipated.

Greatly encouraged, I started practising like a mad thing but circumstances knocked me for six after four months. It was my first year of marriage. I developed a bad dose of flu' over Christmas and when three weeks later I was still flat on my back, there was an urgent call made to the doctor. I had taken a dislike to most cooking smells; I couldn't keep any food down. When the doctor heard this, he asked a few more details, and declared I was pregnant. I was dumbfounded. I wasn't sure to be happy or sad, I was feeling so wretched. I made a slow recovery, all the time feeling desolate within. I felt my life was terribly out of control. I was shocked by my thoughts, so I pushed them into the background.

Eventually, I resumed piano practise, but it wasn't consistent, and finally I sat for the diploma in June '72. Eric took me there on the back of his Lambretta motorcycle, After the exam, Eric gave me the music of "The Lord's Prayer" as a gift expressing his admiration in anticipation of my achievement. He would never know the result.

I learned the results of the diploma five days after Eric's funeral. I had passed the theory section, but failed the practical section. I repeated the practical twice within the twelve-month period, but to no avail. The second time my marks dropped to

62, the third time I gained 8 points coming out with 70. It was five marks less than the pass mark; so near and yet so far. It was a bitter pill to swallow, especially as I was getting remarried and hoped to teach once Eddy and I were settled.

Over in England, the pressure continued. I worked on moulding myself into this image I had of a classical enthusiast. I collected classical records from sales; I mean heavy classical, and operas. I read up on the lives of composers till my brain was addled with all the facts. My new music teacher had me playing Chopin's Minute Waltz that I could never play up to speed, and Mendelssohn's Andante and Rondo Capriccioso that was about a dozen pages long. I was out of my depth. She held music soirees, and encouraged us all to play our favourite pieces to family and friends. It was a great idea to teach us musical appreciation and to learn to conquer nerves. I tried hard to perform, but it was a great strain. One pupil played the "Moonlight" Sonata with effortless ease and I longed to play it just like her. But no matter how much I practised it never flowed together. It was always broken and disjointed.

In private, I was on a constant diet regime, maintaining my weight at a ridiculous level for an active mother, so I was always hungry, always on edge. Occasionally, I would binge (because I was so hungry) for an afternoon while Eddy was at work. Then the next day, I would starve myself to make up for what I considered indulgence. I never considered that due to lack of nourishment I didn't have the stamina for my musical activities, that the lack of food affected my concentration. This was the reality of the situation, but one I could not come to terms with just then and it was something I would never discuss with anyone. I tried the examination for the fourth time that year and failed dismally, for the first time my marks were down in the 40's. The date of the exam and our move to Ireland coincided the same week. It was extremely bad timing. This was the background to the build up of pressure related to the failure in music.

As a single parent, there were some very practical things to take care of that would have thrown me into turmoil, but they were taken in hand by Bob McAlister. He dealt efficiently with all the complexities of filling forms and dealing with the Department of Social Welfare in order to obtain a pension and a flat. For months, he battled with the Welfare system overcoming obstacles. He also gave me driving lessons, his patience and confidence giving me courage to drive. Eddy had tried to teach me while living in the country but I lost my composure when we came across a herd of cows filling the road! I almost felt claustrophobic with those big animals surrounding the car. If I couldn't handle this situation, how could I face the traffic congestion in Dublin, I reasoned. But I needn't have worried with Bob's determination to get me through. If he noticed I was losing my nerve at holding up other drivers while doing a three-point-turn, he'd say: "Don't worry, you paid your road tax just the same as them, so take your time."

While you're in that in-between stage of learning to drive, looking on at the licensed motorists driving sanely and in control, you feel almost a different species to the rest of the human race! I compare the learner driver to a person doing driving stunts in a comedy. You fail to synchronise your movements between the clutch and the accelerator, that the car looks like it has a fit of the hiccups! It lurches and stalls all the way down the road until you feel quite giddy. You're told to do a three-point turn and nearly die with mortification when you do it in six turns. You make the gears grind unmercifully as you flee down

It Happened Again

the road, away from the glares of the waiting motorists. I felt I should be driving one of those old German Messher Schmied bubble cars with balloons tied on, to suit the mood of the occasion! (The Messher Schmied looked like the cockpit of an aeroplane on wheels!) And just when you think you've got the hang of the controls and you're growing almost smug and sure of yourself, you approach a T-Junction. Suddenly, your feet refuse to obey the signals from your brain and you're terrified you're going to crash, finally your foot finds the brake and you're brought to an abrupt stop, you're almost propelled through the windscreen. You're overshooting the stop line.

I failed my first driving test, and was tempted to stop there but Bob said most people fail the first time, and he entered me straightaway for a second test and spent much time in helping me perfect the three-point-turn and hill start. Since I was so nervous at driving the car on my own, (the law had changed for a brief while and people with provisional licences were allowed to drive without a licensed driver to accompany them) I requested God to assign an angel to sit in the passenger seat and keep me safe!

The day dawned bright and fair for the test, the examiner was friendlier than the first one, he set me at ease immediately. After I had driven a couple of miles and carried out the main manoeuvres neatly, he got me to stop the car, and asked me a couple of questions about the Rules of the Road, which I answered satisfactorily. Then he asked me, "Why do you want to drive?" I thought to myself, "What a weird question. Isn't it obvious?" He repeated his question. I replied: "To be independent." He asked again, "Why do you really want to drive?" I thought for a moment, and then told him: "To take my children to school and to visit my parents in the country." (At that time the farm was our refuge to get away from the noise and clamour of the city.) He inquired: "Doesn't your husband drive the children to school?" I explained about my husbands. He inquired the reason for my calm state of mind in the face of such misfortune. How was it that I spoke without bitterness and blaming God? Blame God? I didn't view God as someone who deliberately doled out affliction and tragedy. I knew Him as the One who cared so much for his creation that He came, Himself, to live amongst us and show us His remarkable love that triumphs in the midst of tragedy. As I shared of the hope within me, I smiled inwardly. Here I was in the middle of a driving test talking about my trust in God. He was deeply impressed as I spoke about my Source of help. This examiner was so different to the previous one who was very business-like and distant. This man made me feel as if he had all the time in the world for me. He really wanted to know what made me tick. He was an older man, that seemed to have got passed the surface things of life, and was prepared to probe beneath to focus on what was truly important.

There were no more questions about driving, he told me to return to the Driving School where he handed me my pass certificate with warm congratulations and best wishes for my future. Joy Gray was looking after Eleanor during my test, so when I got to her house I ripped the L- plates off the car, and went into her kitchen dumping them triumphantly amid cries of congratulations from John and Joy.

I determined that I would be prepared for any emergency while travelling. With my first car I had one or two breakdowns, a flat tyre, which was soon put to rights by some helpful motorists that I had waved down. But it was getting a bit dangerous to wave people down (damsel in distress and all that), so I thought it was time I learned to change a wheel myself. I had an Austin Metro by this time, which was nicknamed "the Bread-Basket" by one of the men at church! I discovered a flat tyre one Saturday morning. I took a look at the instructions, to change a wheel, in the driver's manual. I told myself that it was like following instructions for a cake recipe! It was laid out in four steps.

My mother was staying with us at the time, and offered her help. It would have been so easy to let her try it. It was always that way. If she was around, she would take the brunt of things to try to shield me, so I leaned too much on her. This time, I flatly refused; I had to know for myself how to manage. I went outside and laid the manual on the ground beside the car and set about changing the wheel. It was so difficult to remove the bolts, I was growing very hot and I stood on top of the manual, almost obliterating the instructions with dirt from my shoes. I was sorely tempted to call my mother. Finally, the bolts loosened, I heaved a sigh of relief. Standing up to take the spare wheel from the boot, I caught my mother peeping anxiously from behind the net curtain. I ignored her, and continued struggling with the procedure. With the jack packed neatly once more in the boot, I walked into the house in jubilant mood. Mum hugged me, telling me "I found it very hard to stop myself from running out there to help you, when you were struggling with those bolts. I'm very proud of you for persevering!"

When I joined Clasp, the association for Christian Single parents (nowadays it's known as Beulah) and listened to various discussions it made me realise more the increased responsibilities and conflict single mothers face. Single parents experience extreme pressures. The mother assumes the dual role of both father and mother. She was not cut out for the man's role of protector, provider, and spiritual leader of the home. In assuming these responsibilities her task is unenviable. Some days it feels like World War III.

She now has to keep a check on the bank statements, and pay the bills. She has to maintain the outside of the home as well as the inside. If she has a car, she has to wash it every week, and there is no husband to take a turn, unless she can persuade the children to help. Sometimes they are not prepared to drop what they are doing just then, so rather than use up her energy persuading them she goes straight out, herself, to wash the car. I found the children needed a little encouragement by the promise of extra pocket money. It may sound like blackmail, but it got the job done.

The Single mother has to learn to deal with mechanics who sometimes see her coming a mile away, and exploit her lack of car knowledge and charge exorbitant prices for service and parts. For instance I found one day that the car needed new brake shoes on top of the usual service. I was in a dilemma as the mechanic stressed the urgency of the job, the dangers I'd be faced with on the road, and my slim budget. I soon grew wise to their tactics and hunted around for a more reasonable service.

For the mother who accepts the challenge of taking the role of spiritual leader in her home, she immediately comes up against Satan, who "prowls around like a roaring lion looking for someone to devour."[2] He is not a myth, or anything like the medieval picture of a character in a red suit with two horns on his head, and carrying a pitchfork. He is not just an evil influence in a Bible story. He is a very real antagonist for every Christian especially someone vulnerable like a single mother, and she has to learn to be alert and defy his intentions. Satan has

It Happened Again

a habit of homing in on our weakest points and this makes the battle all the harder. For instead of recognising clearly that the attack is spiritual, that the enemy is complicating the situation, the mother often focuses on her weakness and is seriously distracted. Defeat is often inevitable. Until she sees that "we wrestle not against flesh and blood" and that she can be covered in Jesus' righteousness.[3] Only then will she be victorious.

I was learning more the battle between good and evil; I found that Satan was clever in trying to defeat me. He was a threat to my peace. He sought to distract me from my purpose of seeking God and get me caught up with bitterness and self-pity. I had to be firm and regularly choose the former frame of mind.

When the single parent has the full responsibility of disciplining the children, she can be seen as the spoilsport, particularly in the area of monitoring videos and T.V. programmes. Whereas most men have broad shoulders to cope with the children's moaning in this area, they also are less emotional so don't get so easily tangled up in an argument, but the gentle spirit of the mother smarts under the glares of the children. They challenge her authority and her beliefs. I think I found this area the hardest of all. Because it was so difficult, caught up in the battle, to differentiate between my own weakness (wanting to please them, weary at the end of a long day) and the occasions the enemy of my soul interfered. It took many battles before I learned to distinguish the signs. In the meantime, I learned (not without a struggle) to stand back from the children when they reached the teenage years, to give them space to try their wings, make their mistakes, to find God for themselves. It's the hardest thing to watch a child, whom you have protected and cared for over the years, to stand back and allow her to try things, especially those things you know are not going to benefit her life.

1. Drewstown House school

2. Eric and Helen in March 1970

3. Eddy and Helen in August 1978

4. My parents with Esther in September 1972

5. Eddy's parents on their ruby wedding celebration

6. Helen, Esther, Eleanor and Joy on holiday in U.K. in 1985

7. Single mums Monica and May with John and Helen on our wedding day, 29th August 1998

8. Pauline and Brian celebrating their engagement, June 2004
9. Our wedding day, August 1998, with my siblings - Joan, Margaret Helen and Isaac
10. Family group on Joy and Peter's wedding day, September 2001

FIVE

Heaven

FOR SOME PEOPLE who have suffered bereavement, it's important to them to visit the grave of their loved one. This is the way they can work out their grief. One friend told me that he found consolation in visiting his mother's grave and telling her the events of his day. He knew he couldn't communicate with his mother anymore, but it just helped to give expression to his thoughts in this way. For me it wasn't a necessity to visit regularly, because I couldn't identify with the still, inert bodies lying within that grave. I had this picture of Eric and Eddy that they were very much alert and enjoying the delights of heaven.

When Eddy's mother came to Ireland, she liked to visit the grave; sometimes the children came with us on the drive. After that the children suggested themselves, once in a while, on a Sunday afternoon, to visit. Eric and Eddy were both buried in the same grave at Mount Jerome, Harold's cross. Once I had parked the car, the children would run ahead of me to the shop to choose flowers and then we would walk up the tree-lined avenue to the grave. On the way, the children sometimes read the inscriptions on other graves. They would be particularly touched if they read of a child who had died. Some of the graves were very old and the stones crumbling. They thought it was rather spooky, especially as we passed the vaults. The girls would try to get a better view through the grids. They were very curious, they would ask loads of questions about the bodies, and particularly what would they look like after being buried so long? It wasn't until they'd seen the remains of the Crusader in the vaults under St. Michan's church on a school tour years later that they better understood. They came home and exclaimed, " We shook the hand of the Crusader today. It was very eerie down there holding his long thin, skeleton fingers." A few years later, visitors were no longer allowed to hold the hand of this distinguished gentleman because the Crusader's remains were getting very fragile.

When we'd reach the grave in Mount Jerome, the girls would help me arrange the flowers in the vase that Grandma Bowen had placed there. The girls wanted to know, "What is it like in Heaven?" "Is it very different to life here on earth?" Esther said, "I think Heaven must be very boring, people praying and singing all the time." She associated it with church, where you spent time every Sunday praying and singing. On the day of the accident I told them that their Daddy was in Heaven; that I believed he was gone to the special place that Jesus had prepared for those who love Him.[1] Now in the graveyard, in answer to their question I told them what I remembered of the description of heaven in Scripture, the throne of God surrounded with thousands of angels worshipping.[2] I believed that when a person dies, it's like they are sleeping until the coming of the Lord;[3] but their spirit is alive and with the Lord.[4]

I told them it would be a place of great beauty, if they could think of the most beautiful place on earth, then heaven would be a million times more beautiful. Esther still wasn't convinced it was a great place. I reflected on what I had said to them, it wasn't a lot to go on. I found it a bit difficult to convey what I felt and thought about heaven. Of course, how can one write or talk about something they haven't seen? Yet, I couldn't help thinking of it. I had found great comfort in the thought that Eric and Eddy were in a peaceful, happy place. I imagined that to be with Jesus would be the most satisfying thing of all. But to a child this all seemed rather vague. They almost need a visual description to convince them. Jesus made a promise to the thief on the cross, "Today, you will be with me in paradise." What does the word 'paradise' mean? From scripture, we see that God loves gardens. Right back at the beginning of time, there was the perfect garden, the Garden of Eden.

I like to think that Eric and Eddy are in a heaven something like Deerpark in Howth. My connection with that beauty spot is an afternoon I spent in Eric's company during our courtship. We climbed up some steps and followed a path leading steadily upwards. I was unprepared for the sight that met my eyes. I gasped when I saw the thousands of rhododendron trees of which there were many varieties. The colours and fragrances were sensational. It was a heady experience.

The path continued at length, until we saw an opening that led out to a clearing that was not cultivated. It was natural and wild. The sun shone warm upon us as we walked amongst the long grass. We were the only ones in this area, and Eric burst out singing a song we'd learned recently at church. I joined in singing the harmony. Our surroundings stirred us to praise the Creator of all this magnificence. Bees buzzed busily amongst the wild flowers and the birds sang their songs. It was heavenly.

Even when a summer shower occurred we were not disappointed. We ran for shelter into a grove of trees. We found a comfortable, dry nook and sat down to wait for the shower to pass. Eric remarked, "It's a pity we didn't bring a picnic. I'm starving!" I reached into my bag and produced a chunk of wedding cake! Eric laughed at his wish being answered immediately.

"Where did you get it?" he asked.

"It's my sister's wedding cake." (Joan had married Neil in Canada some months previously and had sent us some cake.) We talked about our future together while we munched the cake. It wasn't a lot to satisfy a tall fellow like Eric. He rose to continue the walk, and to get to the shops for some more grub. The rain had passed; we joined the upward path again savouring the scents emanating from the wet soil. Eventually, we reached the top, we were standing on a vast rock with heathers dotted here and there, and beyond that we had a breath-taking view of Howth harbour and the sea. If this beauty spot could be so impressive, what must Heaven be like?

Thinking further about the subject of heaven, I recalled about a month after Eric died, I was going home from church with John and Joy, I was still caught up with the glory of heaven and remarked, "Just think! Eric has been one month in heaven. What must it be like for him?" I longed to know the pleasures he was enjoying. John shared how he had taken Joy and the children to Drewstown during the week. As they were going home in the evening, driving towards the gates there was a beautiful sunset. The sun was just like a great ball of fire in the sky. Pauline, who was about four at the time, shouted from the back seat, "Look! Eric is up there." Pauline had picked up snatches of our conversation about Eric; she associated the glory of the sunset with what she'd heard about heaven, this new place that Eric was living in.

I was preoccupied with heaven. This was my way to cope with bereavement. Even though I had the comfort and Christian hope of seeing Eric and Eddy one day in Heaven; yet I was aware of some tension and discomfort within me at the graveside. I could not face it; doggedly I clung to my thoughts of heaven. Bereavement affects people different ways. My neighbour told me he missed his mother dreadfully, and because he lacked a scriptural background he was considering contacting a medium to make a connection with his mother. He thought it might help him cope with the great loneliness he felt. I sympathised with him, because I knew there is such an overwhelming longing to talk to our loved ones. I showed him the warning in Scripture to avoid such action;[5] I gave him a leaflet about the dangers of mediums. I told him that usually mediums will try to impress the grieving person by telling them what they want to hear, but as the weeks go by the person is drawn into a tangled web of deceit. I had seen this happen when a friend, who lost her husband, consulted a fortune teller. There is another verse that informs us that it is not wise to consult mediums and spiritists. It is better to inquire of God than to consult the dead.[6]

I had read with great interest some accounts of near death experiences; where people have seen themselves leave their sick body behind and they experience great peace, beauty and light. Some heard a voice offering comfort; others claimed they saw angels and heard celestial music.

A friend shared with us how she was ill following childbirth; she felt she had died and left her body and moved upwards towards a bright light. She looked back and saw her still form in the bed, beside her husband. There were two angels in the room and she knew they were coming for her. She could also hear her child crying and said she couldn't go because the child needed her. One of the angels went over and looked towards a bright light coming through the wall and then turned back and said that it was all right for her to go back. She found herself sliding back into her body.

From what I can gather hearing and reading these accounts the transition from one dimension to another is relatively quick and easy. It's like passing from one room to another; it is not something to be afraid of if we trust our Heavenly Father. And if we are seeking to please him here on earth in our daily activities; then it will just be a continuation of this on the other side. We will develop our learning processes and will have a bigger capacity to understand why we exist and the plan of God for eternity.

I'd like to share John's vision of heaven given to him in a dream. He was with a group of people from church and they came across a river, it was beautiful with stones on the bottom. But it had weeds in it, in the form of green matted algae. It had a beauty but it was not perfect. As John was looking at the river, he said to the Lord, "Isn't there a river on this mountain that I could call my own?" Even though it was nice, he wanted something better, a river more fresh and clear. The dream seemed to jump; the view had changed. John was higher up standing on some moorland, and was looking down upon a walled garden.

The dream jumped again. He was standing in front of a pair of huge wrought iron gates. They must have been about 25' high and very ornate. The garden wall was made of intricately patterned brickwork with pillars at intervals adorned with vases from which cascaded streams of flowers. The dream changed again, and John found himself inside a garden looking at avenues of roses; which ascended to form arches 20' in the air.

The columns were a solid mass of neatly trimmed roses; of which four columns came together to form a high arch. He could see whole avenues of these arches going off in different directions.

Hidden in the columns were a multitude of birds because from them you could hear their beautiful song, which blended in with music that seemed to be in the very air. Soft green turf formed pathways beneath the arches. As he listened to the birds and the music, John noticed that there was no melody, no distinct tune or rhythm. It was harmonious, quite different to earthly music. John saw many paths; he knew somehow that one of these paths led to the fountain of living water, for which he was eagerly searching. There were unseen gardeners (angels) working in the place, he couldn't see them but was aware of their presence. John had been given a glorious picture of heaven, something to look forward to in the future. When John tried to describe his dream afterwards, he was very conscious that words were inadequate to explain effectively the beauty and the splendour he had seen.

I was so excited about these things I shared some of it with my Sunday school class; the children were wide-eyed with interest. It was a very practical outworking of my meditations. We sang songs about heaven and there was a lovely atmosphere in the room that day as we discussed the reality of heaven.

SIX

Redirected Love

THERE ARE TREMENDOUS adjustments in adapting to life without a husband. When one has been accustomed to sharing their life with someone else, and enjoying it, losing them leaves an awful sense of incompleteness. To walk alone is extremely painful. Going on a church outing, for instance, can be such an emotional experience. Seeing a husband help his wife set up the picnic table, and fathers play football with their children tears a grieving heart in two. Speaking for myself, I felt as if one half of me had been literally cut off. There was a dreadful sense of loss, not that I would ever have admitted to that feeling at the time. Seven or eight years passed before I'd even say to God:

"I'm a normal, healthy woman, my hormones continue to function, I have all this love inside me to bestow upon some man, but I can't function in the normal way. What am I to do with all this love and energy, how can I cope with my sexual needs?"

I had filled my life with activities to the point of exhaustion, many times, so that wasn't the answer.

A quick answer to this problem is to remarry, but for most

women this depends on her age and circumstances - how many children are dependent on her. It is a common remark from single parents and single girls that there are not enough men to go round! Some women try dating agencies, and although some have been fortunate enough to find a good partner, mostly it is a great risk to apply. You could be bringing unnecessary trouble upon yourself. Lets be real about this. You could be picking up the problem men, for example, the ones who have been so pampered by their mothers that they are just impossible to live with.

Some women are so determined to get a husband they will try every means possible. They will rush quickly into a relationship and not weigh up carefully whether they are compatible. Once they are married, they realise too late, that they have made the wrong choice. Some women try to put pressure on an unsuspecting man and convince him that they have good reasons to marry; the woman may have a strong emotional need and thinks it will be met in a relationship with this man; the man falls for it because he is lonely. Real love doesn't come into the equation; there is no give and take. Very soon, there are terrible arguments and eventually they separate. People get desperate sometimes when they are lonely.

For a time I thought if I could just date someone with whom I could share the same interest; it would be enough. I thought, it's not necessary to think in terms of love and marriage. Very soon I met a musician, and we arranged to have dinner one evening. We had a very interesting conversation over a delicious meal, and I thought to myself, I could get to like this. It was such a pleasure to dress up and be taken out to a fine hotel and treated to the best of everything. Yet at the back of my mind was the thought, this is not going to work. I couldn't trust myself with this kind of arrangement, I sensed that this man was looking for a wife and he would want love to enter the equation at some point; I knew that I couldn't give my heart to him. He was so nice but very puzzled when I said I couldn't meet him again.

There was another time, just out of the blue; I received a phone call from a widower who had seen me briefly on holiday. He made inquiries about me and eventually made contact. He suggested that we take the children on an outing to Pheonix Park. He had a large family; I had a mental picture of me submerged in armloads of washing and ironing. I didn't want to sound uncaring but I told him as tactfully as possible that I was unable to meet him.

It would have been very tempting, in one sense, to get acquainted, for he was a rich farmer and could have given me a secure future; and in return he would have someone to care for his children and help on the farm. The man meant well and obviously was in need, but from my point of view it was unsuitable in every way.

I told my mother about the phone call; we laughed at the idea of me in the role of a busy farmer's wife with children pulling out of me on all sides. Mum said that I would be worked off my feet. She knew I would never fit into that mould. Even when she heard Eddy had ideas of living self-sufficient on an acre of land; and planning to raise chickens; grow vegetables and graze cattle on the land she thought I would be no use to him! She knew me too well, that I just had no inkling for farm work of any kind. They tried to teach me to milk a cow when I was young and do you think I could get milk out of that animal? I sat for ages squeezing the udder, and it just wouldn't come. Mum demonstrated once again and it looked so easy when she did it. I squeezed again with all my might but it was like getting blood from a stone. I jumped off the three-legged stool in frustration and stomped off. That was the end of my farming!

When a girl is preconditioned to marry from childhood, you expect to marry, your whole life and thinking is geared towards that end. It is a very painful thing to come to terms with reality. If death or separation or even a broken engagement has prevented one from living in the married state, then it is necessary to redirect their love and energies into another area. The problem that faces a Christian is the popular trend to have a relationship without getting married. People think it's old-fashioned to uphold the view of sex within marriage. I faced these dilemmas and I realised the strong capacity to love within me could be redirected to God. I weighed this up for some time. I thought, "Could there possibly be another way to live; to feel complete? I felt God offered me a solution; that He was asking me not to follow the way of the crowd. It was these basic thoughts that gave me the ideas for this chapter a long time ago before my book was started. I had to live it out before I could write it. In this chapter I share my discovery of the unconditional love of God directed to me personally, and as I responded to this warm, accepting love I found a new direction for my love.

It was through regular times of worship at home, listening to a music tape, or playing the piano, that I learned how to redirect my love. Reading the life stories of others telling that Jesus filled the void in their lives, encouraged me to find out for myself. He showed me how to focus on Him, get to know Him better and I would find the sense of loss would be replaced by the gift of His love. This did not happen overnight, it was a slow process, over a number of years. Also, admitting my needs helped rather than living in denial. To deny only led to destructive behaviour.

It Happened Again

This is how it worked out in practical terms. I can only explain it in terms of a Christian approach. I discovered, as a result of my regular worship times, that the Holy Spirit made Jesus more real. We all know that music can be very soothing and uplifting to our spirits. Coupled with the Word of God it is a powerful tool to overcome depression.[1] Songs based on scripture especially had this effect on me. I was aware of the power that worship songs had on me, to cut across the heaviness that would descend upon me. And I didn't have to wait until Sunday to experience this power in church; I included worship in my daily quiet time by simply sitting down at the piano to sing a song or play a worship tape. Worship was now appealing and satisfying. I had a craving for deep heart satisfaction and I found it when I drew from the wellspring of life.[2]

It was exciting to find that God actually seeks a relationship with us and because He is a spirit, to experience the Baptism in the Spirit helps us to connect in a vibrant relationship with His spirit. To be filled with the Spirit enriched and encouraged me in my worship. I found worship is a heart relationship with God, something to be experienced, not just to perform out of duty. The living Presence of Jesus captivated my heart. He drew me like a magnet.

I became aware of His Presence even outside of my quiet times. This was shown to me one particularly difficult day. I admitted to God, that as much as I was grateful to Him for His comfort, how could I live without the company of a human being? I loved God but I could not see Him. On this particular day, I had withdrawn into the pages of some novel, when I became aware of Someone in the room. I sensed a gentle touch upon my arm. Soon I was surrounded and enveloped by this Gentle, Irresistible Presence. The book fell to the floor forgotten, tears flowed down my face as I worshipped Jesus in quiet adoration. I began to understand the function of the Holy Spirit better, for now I could see Jesus with the eye of faith. I was experiencing the tangible Presence of Christ.

I learned to distinguish my longings. Not every longing I experienced was for a husband. I reminded myself that even while I was married, I used to have deep longings and could be very frustrated because they were not satisfied. I realised that it's impossible to expect a man to satisfy his wife fully and vice versa. There is a part in every human being that only God can satisfy. This was a turning point for me. I'd go to God and pour out my need; He'd fill the empty space. As I grew to love Him more, I talked less about the need of human companionship.

Of course, there were days that memories would be stirred by a favourite love song played in a supermarket while I shopped, such as "And I love you so" by Perry Como. Eddy had given me the record single during the first year of our marriage. Or I'd catch a glimpse of some man walking down the street whose profile would remind me of Eddy. The effect would be overwhelming.

Then I gained invaluable insight from a conversation with a minister from Australia, visiting our women's Prayer Fellowship; he was talking to Fiona and I over a cup of tea following the main meeting. He asked us both a little about our background. I mentioned that I was widowed with three children.

He spoke of an experience he had one evening while present in a meeting at home in Australia and absent from his wife (he was frequently away on speaking engagements, it could be very lonely sometimes). He told me how the anointing of God was so strong upon him, he was so caught up with the joy and blessing of God that he thought to himself at the close of the meeting: "Who wants a wife when there is this joy and satisfaction in Jesus?" Here was a minister putting his finger on my problem. It is possible to feel so close to Jesus that you don't miss your husband or wife! This kind of plain speaking was a bit thin on the ground. Somehow single parents feel they're left to muddle through in this area, that the church doesn't address it. I thanked God for bringing this man across my path. This brief conversation convinced me that I was right to pursue the Lord, that I would find the answer to my problem.

I read much about Jesus' life and interaction with others. Reading between the lines about his brothers and sisters, there was little support, they misunderstood His mission. In reaching out to people day after day, Jesus, it was said, had no place to lay his head.[3] He did not have a place to call his own. He knew little of home comforts. But there is no one like him; he sympathizes with our weaknesses, he knew what it was like to be tempted; he just never sinned.[4] A friend said to me that this was what drew him to Jesus, the fact that He knew what it was to be tempted. He knows what we're up against.

In my encounter with Jesus, as a teenager, I experienced mostly his forgiving love at first. I responded to Him as I did to most adults, I thought His love was conditional. I knew His commands; and His promises were conditional. So I tried very hard to please Him. He had wiped the slate clean, and I didn't want to spoil it again. I wore myself out, for I hadn't grasped the meaning of Grace. I had a hard time accepting that He forgave over and over again. His promises were mostly conditional but his love was unconditional.

When I realized that Jesus love was unconditional, I began to trust Him more. While I thought it was conditional, I kept Him at a distance, as I did with family and friends. I don't think parents mean to relate to their children on a conditional basis, but it creeps in nevertheless, because they have the responsibility to discipline. The children develop problems when parents offer love conditionally and tend to correct them too often. It doesn't have to be like this with parenting or in approaching God; we can tap into the unconditional love He offers and find our attitudes changing daily.

I asked myself what exactly is unconditional love and I found it is simply love without conditions; readily accepted, love not based on performance. In a performance-conscious society, this is comfort indeed. Unconditional love means to be tolerant with another.

I found the greatest example of unconditional love in the story of the Prodigal son. The father's love was shown in such a compassionate and forgiving manner. When the erring son returned from living a reckless life, the father could have remained aloof furious over the loss of a fortune. Instead, he had been looking out for his absent son and when he saw him approaching so dejectedly, he ran quickly to him and gathered him to his heart and hugged him tightly. He wanted to lavish his love upon him, tell him that all was forgiven. He was beside himself with excitement at his son's return. He wanted to dress him in the best clothes and throw a party. He couldn't do enough to show his rapturous delight and joy over this reunion. He had missed his boy sorely. This was the kind of warmth and love that was conveyed to me as I thought on my glorious heavenly Father. What a big heart of love and affection He possessed![5]

When the penny dropped for me regarding Jesus' love, that it was far, far different to the way I perceived love, I was ready to really get acquainted with Him, to be on intimate terms with him, to pour my love out to Him. And the more I basked in His warm, accepting love the more I felt enabled to direct my love to others.

I couldn't write this chapter without touching this issue of the need for love and sexual needs in some way. I needed answers to a very important question and I found that my friends had the same need while talking to them at Single Parent Weekends. We don't want platitudes. If the subject is handled negatively, then human nature being what it is will resort to negative behaviour. But if people are willing to face the issue then I believe they will find answers.

I am not claiming to know all the answers; I am just making an attempt to face the issue, for I was in that position myself. It is hard to put into words something spiritual but God's Word clinched the matter for me. I found it wasn't just pie in the sky but a workable faith. I discovered that God honours his promises to those who are prepared to seek him.

· SEVEN ·

He will give His angels charge over you

MOVING TO THE MAISONETTE was a major event for me, knowing that the area was rather rough. I was told stories of teenagers joy-riding, frequent car thefts and domestic violence. The reality of the situation was not as bad as some other areas in the city, but for me coming from the country it was a culture shock. There were also horses loose on the roads, belonging to the itinerants. Sometimes you'd see the children riding bareback galloping down the streets with no regard for smaller children. One time, I heard a mother screaming when she walked outside her front door and found a horse blocking her path! It wasn't something I'd fear coming from the country, but the city-born mother was shaking.

At night I felt defenceless without the strong presence of a man in the house. I turned to the Psalms for comfort, "For He will command his angels concerning you to guard you in all your ways."[1] "The angel of the Lord encamps around those who fear him, and he delivers them."[2] I prayed that God would put his angels round about our house.

It Happened Again

Bill Turner visited our fellowship again, and while I consulted him for counsel and prayer, he touched on the question of angels without me saying anything. While exercising his prophetic gifting he detected my vulnerable point, prayed for God's protection upon the children and me. Then he told me that he could see an angel sitting on my right side! As we sat quietly in prayer, I became aware of someone touching me, supporting me on my shoulder. This was new, it was startling, and I didn't know you could experience God's promises to this degree. I was greatly comforted; God had witnessed the loneliness, the big gap in our home, the environment we lived in fraught with uncertain dangers. I read up a lot about angels, and found out that they surround the throne of God day and night and they are ministering spirits sent to wait on and help God's people.[3]

When I was alone, I felt exposed to all sorts of pressures - financial, moral, and social. And there have been times, in extreme testing, that I've sensed a heavenly being grip my arm or hand and hold it firmly, that I was in no doubt that I was completely safe.

Naturally, I would have liked to see these angels for myself but to see them is not the purpose they visit. There is a growing interest in angels today, where some people seek and exalt them above God, they are not to be worshipped for God created them.[4] I realized the one thing to be aware of is that Satan was once an angel, and when he rebelled he was thrown out of heaven with a third of the angels. They work against the Kingdom of God; some even appearing as angels of light.[5]

When some friends told me about angels visiting them I noticed in some accounts that the angels were dressed in white robes, complete with long hair and wings and sometimes a

He will give His angels charge over you

bright light would shine around them. For others the angels appeared as very ordinary people; wearing ordinary clothes. My experience was mostly a warning thought that caught my attention; and later on when the danger was over I would be aware that angels had kept us safe.

One Sunday afternoon, as we returned from church, I had the distinct impression not to park the car up the laneway beside our gate. I thought it was strange because the only alternative was to park it down on the road, partly on the curb. I asked God to protect it and went inside to prepare the dinner. Later on in the evening, there was some commotion outside with our neighbours in the downstairs Maisonette opposite us. The man seemed to be having trouble with his car; a rusty battered Renault 4. All of a sudden there was an explosion, and a big shout as the man darted away from his car. The car was lifted up in the air with the force of the bang and it landed down right in the spot where my car was usually parked. By this time the Renault was in flames.

The noise and flames frightened my girls but I reminded them that the angels were with us protecting us; we had nothing to worry about. None of the loose fragments from the car had hit the windows of our flat or those of our neighbours and our car was safe down on the curb. Silently, I was thanking God for the direction he had given me earlier in the day.

I thought back to when Eric was alive and an incident that took place on a snowy night in December. Eric and I were returning from a day in Dublin where Eric had preached at the morning and evening services, we were going back to the farm to continue our Christmas holidays. Eric was driving our pastor's Volkswagen minibus, and we took the North road, turning off for Kentstown and Navan. It had been snowing during the day, but by evening the weather had got worse. Eric still decided to drive, but a few miles down the road I was growing anxious as blizzard conditions developed.

As we rounded a bend we came across a fork in the road, Eric mistakenly took the left fork and then realised he was wrong. He swerved to get on the right fork but couldn't control the steering. The van went into a skid and we were heading straight for the ditch. The impact would be serious especially on my side. Amazingly and abruptly, the van came out of the skid and Eric faced it on the right fork and we proceeded for Navan. We were silent after such a narrow escape, both busy with our own thoughts. I felt winded, like someone had kicked me in the stomach. With such a sudden swerve and the icy conditions we should have crashed. I think the angels must have had to move very fast that night to keep the van from overturning.

In Nov '91, the children and I were returning from a day at the farm, and had just reached the outskirts of the city when I saw a car coming out from a side road. The driver didn't see me approaching, he just continued moving out. I knew there would be a collision yet I felt paralysed to do anything, when clear as a bell; the thought came to me to swing over quickly. It cut across my thoughts; I knew it was the Holy Spirit urging me into action. I swung the car over to a piece of waste ground. I stopped the car and rested my head on the steering wheel a moment; so glad we were safe. Then voices started calling to me, one was the driver of a bus parked at a bus stop opposite. He was asking me if we were all right. Then the driver of the car came rushing across the road and apologised over and over for not looking to his left before moving out on the main road. I assured them that we were fine; we were shaken but all right. We had no insurance matters to sort out. It was apparent there were angels around that night saving us from a fateful accident.

There are many accounts of sudden angel appearances out of nowhere and when the danger has passed they just as suddenly disappeared. When I shared my convictions with my sister, Joan, one year she was home from Canada, I found she too relied on God's promise about angels. She is convinced that an angel took care of her when she was very sick on the ferry crossing between England and Ireland, when her boys were small. She was so unsteady with seasickness that she was swaying in the aisles, trying to get to the cafeteria. A young man offered to help her there, and then said he'd look after Jarrod and Brett while she rested. He was true to his word, and when she turned round to thank him on arrival in Dublin port, he was gone!

There is growing interest in the supernatural. Many people presume the supernatural occurrences in their lives are all from God. This is not necessarily true. At a time when God is moving by His Spirit, Satan is busy with his counterfeits. Some angel stories do not line up with the Word of God. I ignore the stories that describe angels as female. The descriptions of angels given in Scripture are always masculine. We've all seen TV. Serials like "Highway to Heaven" starring Michael Landon and films that give us the idea that we'll be angels in heaven after death. It's a nice sentimental thought, but not accurate. God has His quota of heavenly hosts.

We will have another role to play in heaven. We will be like the angels of heaven in the sense that we will not exist in a married state, (if we were married on earth) for there is no marriage in heaven.[6] I know this will come as a shock to some married couples that can't imagine existing any other way. How will we relate to our spouse in that new life? For what it's worth, I think it is hard for us to comprehend such things with our finite minds but when we reach Heaven our knowledge and experience will be so expanded; our minds will be better able to accept our new situation.[7] Our heart's devotion will be focused, unselfishly, on loving and serving Jesus, we will be so secure in this love that our relationships with each other will be on a different level, we will not feel threatened that it is different.

In the last days, there will be increased visitations of angels. I am mindful of the fact that the counterfeit will be in operation in an attempt to undermine God's purposes. You may ask why I make references to the last days. The thought may scare you but that is far from my intention. I wish only to comfort, as I was comforted, and prepare people for these times ahead. The reason I mention the last days is because I believe there are signs occurring that show they are approaching. Jesus talked about the signs of the end of the Age.[8] Briefly, the signs are: wars, and rumours of wars; famines; earthquakes and pestilences, all kinds of fearful events. We are all familiar with the pictures of earthquakes, severe flooding; foot and mouth disease; terrorist attacks; anthrax scares etc. on our television screens. Many will turn from their faith; false prophets and false Christs will appear. But Jesus tells us *not to be troubled*, He urges us to be watchful, not to be deceived. And when He finally returns, everyone will know, for He will send His angels to gather His people from the four corners of the earth.

· EIGHT ·

Tidings of comfort and joy

WHEN WE THINK of Christmas our first thought is fairy lights and tinsel, mince pies and pudding, glowing fires and family. Yet for many families it is the saddest time of the year due to financial pressure or the loss of a loved one, or an excess of alcohol. As a single parent, Christmas for me was a nightmare in the early days. When the children asked, "Mammy, when are we getting our Christmas tree?" All I wanted to do was kick the tree as far as Timbuktu! The thought of all the fuss, the endless work, the cleaning and baking, made me tired before I even started. The standard around my area was a great big house cleaning much like a Spring-cleaning. The whole house had to be scrubbed from top to bottom, this meant that curtains were taken down, and windows washed. Then the shopping had to be planned. Each child had to be clothed from the skin out in new garments. Not just a new dress or a sweater but a whole outfit!

A lot of my trouble was simply the absence of a husband to join in the fun and the planning. Eric and Eddy had always been very involved in these occasions. My negative reactions stemmed from my childhood experience of Christmas. I may

It Happened Again

have had a father but he didn't laugh at Christmas, or gather round the table with us to plan the event. He always seemed to be absent when we most needed him. It was my mother who made Christmas for us. It was she who did all the washing, ironing, baking, and shopping, on top of her farm jobs. She had so much to do that she usually decorated the tree late Christmas Eve with our help and was wrapping presents way after midnight. On Christmas day, Dad sat like a lord at the head of the table waiting to be served dinner. It was the old Victorian way that a man had nothing to do with the kitchen work. I guess the men thought they did enough work outside. I wouldn't have minded that so much if only Dad was not so withdrawn and tense on this special occasion.

Now, here I was, a Single parent and I was determined to make Christmas a great time for my children, even though I, too, ended up decorating the tree late Christmas Eve and wrapping presents way beyond midnight that I usually ran into Santa Claus as he dropped a few presents on the children's beds! There wasn't much sleep those nights. The greatest pressure was the high expectations put on mothers when buying gifts for their offspring; brand new bicycles, Cindy dolls with all their paraphernalia.

I saw one of my neighbours scrimp and save to put a deposit down on a bicycle that cost a hundred pounds and struggle for the rest of the year with the payments. That was a lot of money in 1980. Many parents bought costly gifts that left them deprived for months after. Some of these parents were single like myself; others had husbands who drank a good deal of the weekly wage. No wonder, when it was all over and the kids were back at school, that us mothers were ready to fall into bed! The refrain of one Christmas carol goes like this: "O tidings of comfort and joy...." For most of us mothers, Christmas was more like tidings of pain and regret.

Eddy and I had once got into debt at Christmas while living in London. Everything was extra expensive. And we lived on soups and quiches for months after. We hadn't greens with our dinner in ages, so seeing some nettles under the trees opposite our living room window I went out and picked them. Served up with quiche that evening they tasted like cabbage. We couldn't afford to buy meat or even greens sometimes and we were behind with our bills. I was not going to allow that to happen again. I couldn't cope with living on the edge, fearing that someone would come knocking on the door looking for payment. So I tried hard to keep within my budget even if it meant the children complaining because they couldn't have the latest model in bicycles and the trendiest dolls. The girls quite understood once I tried to explain to them how things were, and their eyes would light up with excitement and appreciation when they opened their gifts. I usually tried to buy them some game or toy that they had hinted about, but that wouldn't break the bank.

One year, I gave Joy a glamorous Cindy doll in a shiny crystal dress with all the accessories but she had to wait awhile to get extra clothes. Grandparents are great people for surprises and the girls were thrilled when they received some Cindy furniture from my mother. Then during the year a huge parcel arrived from England with extra dolls, clothes and furniture including a Cindy car that Grandma had picked up in a sale.

One Christmas Eve it was emphasized to me how blessed my girls were despite our circumstances. We were going to the farm for Christmas and I had loaded up the Triumph with cases and presents. Outside Navan, I got a puncture and when I raised the lid of the boot to get out the spare wheel, I realised I had to unload our luggage and the pile of presents. Lifting all those presents out on a wet, dark night by the side of the road made me groan. But I had a change of heart as I considered the amount of presents my girls would be opening the following day. As I placed them back in the boot, I couldn't help but be thankful for the friends and relatives who helped to brighten up the children's Christmas. They never lacked at Christmas. When the girls talk of those times now, they say that they never felt deprived.

I viewed Christmas with mixed feelings for another reason - all the festivities, all that food. An anorexic person and Christmas just don't get on. I loved bread stuffing and Christmas pudding, mince pies, the lot, but even as I would be eating I'd think "I'm going to weigh a ton when all this is over." The women's magazines don't help when they feature wonderful diets in the weeks leading up to Christmas. It's crazy really, people go on a diet before Christmas, and then they put back all the pounds over the festive season. Well, this is what I did, and the daft thing was I didn't need to lose any weight. But I would be watching my diet while racing around preparing for the holiday, and taking care of three lively youngsters. I was half starved, and wouldn't admit it.

I went to the Post Office one day to get my pension and post my mountain of Christmas cards, and there was a queue of people all the way to the door and out to the pavement. I couldn't go off and come back when there were less people around; I needed money immediately for shopping. So there I was in the queue, starving, and my head full of the list of things I had to do that day. I wondered why my back was aching so badly, and then all of a sudden it got worse and I thought to myself, I'm not going to be able to stand up straight here. I felt like keeling over. Once I got my money I was in no shape for shopping, I needed sustenance and just bought the basic necessities and went home and had some lunch. Did it teach me a lesson? Not at all, I put myself through the same torture the next day. And kept it up until I got home to the farm.

While my mother helped me unpack the car, she kept looking at me strangely. She was talking happily about how good it was to have us home again, while I could hardly see straight. While we settled the children to bed, I longed to roll into bed too and not wake up until the whole fuss and kafuffle was over. Mum suggested a cup of tea, which I accepted but there wasn't much talk out of me that night. A few nights later, she remarked, "Oh you are much more relaxed tonight. When you came first, you seemed very tense, and your eyes were glazed." She was right; my manner was so stiff, like an automaton, with the excessive pressures.

One Christmas, feeling emotionally ragged, wondering how I was going to get through another year of the same endless routine I came across some verses in a Psalm that talked about refreshing in the midst of a wasteland.[1] Christmas can feel very much like a wasteland, a dry and lonely place to someone still suffering the effects of bereavement. Traditional things offer small comfort when you've lost so much. What I needed now was someone who could dispel my sadness and quieten my inner turmoil. I wanted something that could satisfy more than the trivia and "peace and goodwill" at Christmas. My experience was usually burnout during this season.

Where was the real meaning of Christmas? Looking again at the Psalm my eyes fell on the words, "God our Saviour, who daily bears our burdens." I remembered that the babe in Bethlehem had come to be my Saviour; He once stood in a place of weakness and loneliness. I took the words of the Psalm at face value and simply asked Him to bear my burden. As I waited before Him, I felt the weight being lifted off. In the days that followed I went about my Christmas preparations with a light heart; and into my thoughts the words of a poem began to form:

> VISIT IN THE SANCTUARY
> In the rush and fuss of Christmas
> I turn aside to whisper
> To God who is my shelter
> My Counsel and Protector.
> He daily bears my burdens
> And covers *all* my stress.
> The wasteland of tradition
> Can't invade my peace of mind
> For I visit in the Sanctuary
> With the Source of quietness.

This insight helped me focus on the true meaning of Christmas. In the following years, sometimes I made great progress and other times I went backwards. It took a great deal of commitment to have a healthy attitude towards a season fraught with stress.

·⁓ NINE ⁓·

Promise of provision

I GAINED GREAT COMFORT and my faith was strengthened when I relied on God's provision when my resources were low. I think it had a profound effect on me that I could receive personal revelation concerning provision from God. It's not just our ministers who can receive insight but the average person can also receive. I was thrown on God's mercy, and needed input to survive. I needed to know God deeply for myself. Not just at church but in the routine of daily life.

I want to share some of God's supernatural care for us, which was really wonderful. Yet the greatest thing of all was not just the things He gave us, but the lasting impression that I was within His view and His loving care.

God's care was extended to us in extreme financial need. On the day of Eddy's accident, his boss handed me his wages that amounted to sixty-five pounds. That was the sum total of our finances. I thought of the insurance policy we had cashed to help us move to Ireland, I regretted that decision. How badly we needed that money now. I had to bear the consequences of that decision yet within a month I received a large cheque for three hundred pounds from the prayer group in England where we used to fellowship. Also Eddy's Mum had taken out an insurance policy for Eddy some years before and it had now matured. These gifts took care of the funeral bills and other things besides. An anonymous gift was given to buy a buggy for Eleanor; someone else loaned her a pram. Further gifts came in, making it possible to purchase a second hand car. I bought a brown shiny TRIUMPH DOLOMITE that looked like new.

In 1983, a promise stood out in my morning reading that God would restore to me twice as much as I had lost.[1] The first major provision was the purchasing of a house. It came about in this manner. On my own, with only a Widow's pension; a small benefit from England and limited income from teaching I could not pay a mortgage. There was the question of compensation from Eddy's employers but it was proving to be very complicated. It was a long drawn out affair, with constant telephone calls and visits to my solicitor's office and wrangling between him and the employer's solicitor. It was somewhat wearying to keep up with the legal jargon and the uncertainty, but mostly, I took it in my stride because I had a good support system from my family and friends.

It took five years to bring the case to court because the facts were so unclear; there were no witnesses at the scene of the accident. It was argued that Eddy had neglected to secure the handbrake adequately on the lorry. Around 1982, I was offered six thousand pounds. My solicitor advised me not to accept it, it was such an inadequate sum, but warned me that if the case came to court I could win a larger sum or nothing at all. My Dad maintained that Eddy was the breadwinner of the family, and as he had died in his boss' employ, I should be awarded at least fifty thousand pounds! I prayed about it and told my solicitor I'd wait for the court case to take place.

Two years later, the case finally came up. On the Saturday

before, these questions came to my mind: How much can you believe for? Can you believe for fifty thousand pounds? No. Can you believe for forty thousand? No. What about thirty thousand pounds? No, I can believe for twenty thousands pounds. It was like a Voice was speaking to me, and I was being realistic with my responses because I knew the arguments the solicitor had posed to me.

When I arrived at the Dublin's Four Courts on the Wednesday morning, with my father and Eddy's parents, there was a long delay. I was told to get some facts together as to how we used Eddy's income each week, so I was nervous about standing up in the witness box before a whole row of stern-faced barristers in wigs and long flowing robes. I was frantically trying to remember back five years, and jot down some figures when my solicitor came running up to tell me an offer of twenty thousand pounds had been made. They wanted to know would I accept? Incredible! Twenty thousand!!! The very sum I said I could believe for on Saturday morning. Naturally, I accepted and the whole thing was settled quickly in the courtroom. I didn't have to face the witness box.

One thousand pounds each was put in trust for the girls until they reached the age of eighteen. I walked away from the Court with my family feeling uplifted at the outcome, but I noticed my father-in-law was struggling with tears. Perhaps it was all too much for him reminding him of Eddy, but when we asked him why he was upset he remarked that the Court case was all over and they probably wouldn't see us again. I tucked my arm within his as we walked together and assured him that this would not happen; we needed to keep in touch, the children needed their grandparents. It was important to keep the family link on their father's side. It was easy to communicate with

Mum Bowen; she has always been open and welcoming. Dad was not so easy to communicate with; nevertheless I wanted to keep the contact. Mum has always been a great example of perseverance and optimism in the face of difficulties.

Twenty thousand wasn't a lot in practical terms. I didn't think it was enough to buy a house. Perhaps if I had exercised more faith I would have got it? But like I say, I knew the arguments related to the case, and it was certainly better than six thousand. That was as far as my faith would stretch under pressure.

I hadn't a clue about the price of houses. I decided that when I went out for a walk everyday, I'd visit estate agents and gain some information. Then, I combed our area looking for a suitable house. I didn't want to move to another area, the children were happy at school. I was drawn to a simple terraced house with four bedrooms; (there were really three bedrooms with a partition wall fixed in to divide the biggest bedroom). There was solid fuel central heating and a phone installed. The price was £22,500. There was a small front garden and a larger one at the back. This was just what we wanted; we were so cramped in the two-bedroom flat and the open garden where all the kids, dogs and even horses of the neighbourhood seemed to jump across! We longed for some place private and this small house seemed just right. But I didn't have £22,500, only £17,000 now that some had been put aside for the girls. Still, considering I got a substantial amount through the courts, my faith was growing speedily. I believed God would take care of the rest.

I made an offer for £22,000 even though I was short about ten thousand pounds to cover the price of the house and solicitor's fees etc. Then God started turning the wheels to release finance. Eddy's father told me he would loan me five thousand,

and I received a further five thousand from Dublin Corporation; not a loan but a lump sum; to enable tenants living in Maisonettes to buy houses. Eric's mother died that February; I received just over a thousand pounds and the contents of her house. A lump sum was left in trust for Esther. I was astonished to hear of these arrangements, because I had never expected any supply from this quarter, because Eric's father was so bitter. The reason that we did receive anything was because the father died first, and therefore the mother who was more softhearted remembered her son's widow and daughter. The extra furniture would come in handy moving from a flat to a house.

I first viewed the house in November 1984 and we moved in April 1985. We were thrilled with all the extra space. It was early May and the weather was very warm and the children enjoyed having meals in the garden without the whole neighbourhood joining us. My father-in-law also moved house that summer and he made such a profit that he told me not to worry about paying back the loan. It had all worked out so wonderfully, I had received enough money to purchase the house, pay a surveyor, solicitor's fees and estate agents.

·⁓ TEN ⌣·

I dare to dream

I WAS CONTENT for many years busy with my children, teaching, and being involved with various activities in our church. Then an idea or impression grew in my heart that I would move to the country, and open my home to give Bible studies. Another idea was also beginning to grow in my mind and heart that seemed just too wonderful for words.

I first began to pray for a partner about eighteen months after Eddy's death. The summer of 1980 was, outwardly, a happy time. There was a family reunion. My sisters, Joan and Margaret, came home from Canada and England with their children and we all gravitated towards the farm. Once again the old house was teeming with life.

One afternoon, unexpectedly, I found I had a quiet half hour. A hush hung over the big house. I had volunteered to wash up the dinner dishes; Mum was resting upstairs, while Eleanor slept in her cot. Joan and Margaret had taken the rest of the children to the swimming pool in Kells. I was thinking how mundane life would be when the summer was over. My sisters, with their children, would return to their husbands and their homes while I would return with my girls to a small flat with no husband and father to greet us.

Once the dishes were washed, I sat down on the wooden bench by the window and tentatively asked God if it were possible that I could marry again. One part of me was aware that now I had three children; that fact would be a stumbling block. The other part of me was feeling lonely and vulnerable, needing desperately the love and support of a husband. The thought went through my mind to wait until Eleanor was grown up. My mind started to work out how long that would be - at least eighteen years.

I wasn't quite sure whether it was God telling me to wait, yet I had asked him a question. I wasn't accustomed to distinguishing His voice clearly at this point of my life. To be truthful, I didn't like to be told to wait, eighteen years seemed a very long time. How would I cope for that length of time? It looked like I would have to bring the children up on my own. It was a very sobering moment. It would have saved me a lot of pain if I had accepted the thought with more grace and committed it to God's keeping. I was unable to accept it at that stage.

From time to time, I received assurances that my circumstances would change. I was told to remain faithful and He would make up the loss. This was also in 1983, when I was drawn to the promise that God was going to bless me with twice as much as I had lost.[1] I was reluctant to read too much into this, that the promise could include a husband. My faith could rise to believe for a home of my own, but at this time, I couldn't believe for a husband. My thinking was undergoing a change. Over the next few years, I grew tired of making feverish demands of God. The up and down (roller coaster) effects were draining my system. By 1990, I gave up struggling about my single state. I felt I could relinquish my hopes. I noticed that prayer was taking on an added quality, I was coming to the point of wanting God's will more than my own.

For about eighteen months I had relinquished the desire to marry. It was in Dec'91 that I sensed a choice was laid before me. He wanted to find out my real feelings on the matter. There were strange stirrings in my heart. I didn't want to start thinking about marriage again unless God was really in it. I found as the days passed, that God was definitely asking me to make a choice. Which way do I want to live - to be single or married? Could I cope with this solitary life after the children leave home? I was capable of growing too introspective.

I really considered practical issues as well. I weighed up the possibilities of losing my independence and losing my own bedroom. These were benefits of the single life that I had grown to appreciate. My bedroom had become my sanctuary, especially early morning meeting with God before the busy demands of the day. Regarding my independence, it depended how one looked at it - if I was marrying for the mutual benefit of my partner and myself I wouldn't see it as a negative thing, and regarding the loss of my own bedroom, I could arrange for a study room, or convert the attic, to foster the relationship I had with God, and the need for my own space.

The whole purpose that God led me in this kind of prayer was to see my real heart and motives. Bit by bit, the layers covering my motives were peeled off over the years until I prayed with the true motive. I had prayed many times for a husband with mixed motives. Finally, God was getting to the heart of the matter.

I was honest with God, I told Him that I wanted to live in the country and help to spread the spiritual blessings we enjoyed in the city, adding that I didn't feel I could live in the country on my own. Close friends said that I was too quiet a person to live alone, and I would turn into a recluse! I needed a helpmate. I told God that if the partner didn't show up I would try to go alone, or perhaps He might think of sending some single people of like mind to help me. After this, it was impressed upon me to pray definitely for a partner. I had the impression of a happy ending. And this was the third time Job's story was brought to my attention. I observed regarding Job's life that after he endured the time of testing he was blessed with twice as much as he owned before the tragedy. Job's end was better than his beginning. He couldn't see what lay ahead. He could only hang on to God's mercy. I too had been severely tested and out of that testing promises had been given to me that over the years had formed the foundation of my faith. I couldn't see what lay ahead; it was a faith venture. Now it was beginning to unfold with the promise of marriage.

The revelation was so clear I reckoned the event would take place very soon. I was very preoccupied with it and found myself listing my requirements for a husband:

1. A godly man
2. Tall (but not a vital requirement), good looking.
3. To have a sense of humour.
4. To have knowledge of music and an instrument, even if he doesn't play regularly. He must be a true worshipper and share the same vision.
5. To have the capacity to cherish his wife, so that the love is reflected in her face. (The reason I put it like this is because Eric told me once how he was so impressed with a married couple, mutual friends of ours, where this cherishing was very evident. It was something we wanted to cultivate.)
6. To be interested in D.I.Y. and gardening.

7. To be a few years older than myself. A widower, used to children. If he has children, I would prefer they are grown up. I don't want to start mothering again.
8. To be good at Maths to help Eleanor. To be active in some sports especially for Eleanor's benefit. To know how to fly a kite! Eleanor would be thrilled.

This last requirement was for Eleanor, as I've said, because she was 12 yrs. old when I made this list, and could really have done with a father around the place, for she was a real tomboy.

I was an incurable romantic, despite the tragedies in troubled marriages I had witnessed, I believed that God had ordained that I would find true romance again. So I was on the look out for this man, not in an obvious way, but nevertheless looking and praying. Seven months later, I went on a holiday to Co. Clare without the girls. Esther was working, the other two were at camp. Surely this would be the time to meet this man! Well, nothing happened during the holiday, and regretfully I boarded the bus back to Dublin. I had set myself up for disappointment, ignoring the inner voice that was saying, "It's not your desire and planning that will bring things about, but My leading entirely."

I remonstrated with myself afterwards, and then laughed at my over-active imagination. I hoped I was cured, that I'd settle down and leave the timing to Providence. I wish I could say that the experience taught me a lesson. Yes, for a time I got busy with music interests and church activities. But "hope deferred makes the heart sick." as the proverb says, and I had to work very hard to school my thoughts.[2] I even forgot my list of requirements asking for a widower, I would have been thankful to meet a suitable single man at this point. After a few relapses, I took my list to God once again and managed to commit my impatience to Him.

I dare to dream

I couldn't keep my thoughts completely from the girls, because Joy joked one evening when I had Liver Casserole for dinner, "If you marry again, I hope your new husband likes liver." We laughed so much over this remark. They loved to tease me whenever I made a small casserole of liver for myself. They thought liver was dreadful stuff, and refused to eat it. Joy wondered if I was on a special diet, she thought I might be deficient in iron. Seeing Joy had brought up the subject of marriage, I wondered if I'd take this opportunity to see what they thought of the idea. So in a casual manner I asked them. Joy had no doubts; she would accept it even if she were still living at home. Eleanor wasn't keen. She was twelve years old and happy with the way things were with the three of us living together. Esther was nursing in England.

I teased Eleanor, asking, "What if he could fly a kite? Would you change your mind?" She was really keen on flying a kite during this phase and wanted somebody extremely patient to help her handle it. I had no patience when it came to untangling knots in the kite strings, and no feel for testing the wind and helping a kite become airborne. Some mortals have endless patience with these things; clearly I was not one of them. In answer to my question she replied, "No, definitely not." I tried again. "What if he was interested in Gymnastics?" She hesitated, then reluctantly replied, "Well...maybe." Gymnastics was another favourite pastime during her first year in Secondary school. Eleanor closed the conversation with the comment, "If you do marry, I won't call him Dad, I will call him by his Christian name." That was fine by me.

I couldn't ask Esther her opinion just then, but she was home later in the year and confided that she started praying around December '91 that I would meet someone and marry

It Happened Again

again. Esther had begun dating so it was dawning on her what I was missing. When she shared this thought I was amazed at the timing; it was the very same month that God led me to pray!

A few months later, the subject came up again. Eleanor was warming to the idea; it pleased her to think of me meeting someone who was into sports. But she told me her objections, her doubts about the whole thing. The main one was the same point I sometimes struggled with - to have a third husband, surely it was too much to expect? She put the question to me, "Doesn't it seem greedy to ask for another? And what if he dies too?" I told her that it was God's idea to prompt me to pray, surely He'd order events and give us a reasonable time together before that event? (Although I must add here that I didn't want to presume either, knowing how suddenly I lost Eric and Eddy.) Having been serious for a while, Eleanor suddenly got playful again, and commented, "Joy might fall in love with him." Immediately, Joy shouted back, "He'll probably be about 60!" At this we fell about the place laughing.

The years rolled on and the promised husband didn't show up. I had to learn to wait patiently; which none of us submit to easily. In my case the girls used to laugh at me; I was so convinced about getting married again and moving to the country. Because there was a delay, they'd say, "Yes, Mum, we'll believe it when we see it."

And still I waited and waited. Then I tried to bring about the reality of my vision. I was always reading the Property magazine wondering if it were possible to buy a small house in the country. When my brother, Isaac, saw my interest, he offered me a field pleasantly situated by the river; although the far side of the field tended to flood in wet weather. I would have had to pay a lot on drainage. A friend got designs of houses from the

Home Exhibition in the R.D.S. as she, too, had dreams of building a house. I looked through the designs and saw one for a simple two-bedroom bungalow, with space in the roof to convert the attic if so desired.

I discussed building a bungalow with Isaac who got in touch with the Planning Authority, talked with a surveyor who said he'd come out to talk with us and view the land. There were long delays, when eventually a time was arranged and I travelled to the farm to keep the appointment. We waited around all day to see this fellow, busying ourselves with clearing out Mum and Dad's belongings, and when he failed to turn up I returned to the city very disheartened. On the journey home, I had the distinct awareness that I was to go no further with this plan. It was the hardest thing for me to put the vision on the " back burner" as it were.

A few days later, I was speaking with Annmarie, a friend at College, who told me how she had to be careful to focus only on the pure vision God had revealed to her for her own life. It is very easy to embellish the message or impression and fill up the blanks with our own thoughts and longings. I was pulled up short by her words. I realised that I had added to the basic vision that God had given me and had convinced myself that there was a door of opportunity for me in my brother's area.

I dared to believe that God would give me the desire of my heart. It was a precious thing to have a dream, or goal, to motivate and give me something to live for. It was important to me to hold onto my dream no matter how tempted I was to lay it aside, through fear of the unknown or through fear of weaknesses, or through friends or family throwing a dampener on them. Even the lack of finance could cause me to give up my dream but I wasn't going to let it stop me.

I had a dream or vision, as I said, that one day I would live in the country and open my home to needy people, I believed I would be given a helpmate to share the work. Outwardly, there was little chance of this, especially about a helpmate.

I remember seeing Martin Luther King on TV, (a repeat documentary) and being moved tremendously when he declared, "I have a dream." His words rang with confidence, excitement, hope, and determination. Some of us may not have such a public dream as he had, but the point is, all of us may have a dream, and become a person of influence in the community where we live.

I'm not saying that every widow and single parent should have a dream of getting married again, life is not like that, what I am saying is, it is possible for us all to have a dream to live a fulfilled, satisfied life. It is possible to have this in a relationship with God and His Son, Jesus, as I've said, for He made us and knows all about us and He understands us completely. Within each of us lies the potential, through the guidance of the Holy Spirit, to find a purpose in life and live it to the full. I've seen women move away from depression and despair to attend courses on different subjects with the view to integrating into society on completion. Some take up teaching or counselling, or get involved with the outreach team in their church. Some advertise for lodgers and make use of the space now that the children have left home. I know one woman who has trained and is now working with the view to owning her own Christian bookshop one day. What a tremendous goal to work towards, this person is an inspiration to us all.

Over and over, when the doubts would surface, I would be reminded of the promise. In a real sense, I was very much aware of the word of God testing me. It is the hardest thing to wait for the word of God to be fulfilled, when the days drag slowly. Most days it was sheer plodding, gritting my teeth as it were, in the face of great testing, and then God would reassure me of the promise and lighten my heart and set me on my way again. It was this constant reassurance of the promise that kept me going. It often felt like I was pestering the Almighty but still He reassured me and strengthened me.

· ELEVEN ·

Emotional Healing

IN ORDER TO PROGRESS in my life, it was necessary to be healed first. It was good, in a sense, that there was a delay to the fulfilment of the promises in order that I might be built up and made strong emotionally. I want to share the healing which I received connected to the eating disorder; my inability to communicate clearly; an orphan spirit; repressed grief; failure; and finally living by a code of rules. These emotional hang-ups strangled any life and creativity that I sought to be produced in me. The six areas of healing are not necessarily in chronological order, for they actually overlapped at times. Indeed, they were all linked to each other. The anorexia was a symptom of the other areas. I believe that these were things of my past that needed to be discarded but they had the potential to re-emerge.

It's not that I dwelled much on these areas, or dug into the past and came up with all these complications I mention in the following pages. I led a busy life looking after my three children, there was not much time for reflection; until I was faced with the situation of being a redundant Mum, when Eleanor went through an identity crisis at the age of 14, and a few years later I faced the Empty Nest Syndrome.

With most bereaved people they usually go through a period of mourning during the first two to three years. With me, there was an outward time of mourning during the funerals and immediately after, and outward adjustments were made, but the grieving process was delayed until the children started to leave home. In the middle stage of the process I was quite broken. It just seemed to be a time of great change in many ways, my mother had developed Alzheimer's and I missed her steady support terribly; and there were changes in friendships especially with Fiona whom I had worked closely with in Sunday school and worship groups for years. Fiona moved to another church and was caught up in different events. It was a dark, lonely period. If anything, it was worse than when the tragedies occurred. It seemed that I was being weaned off every prop that I had ever leaned upon.

The Holy Spirit initiated the healing and drew my attention to the areas I will discuss in this chapter. He revealed that it was God's intention to loose me from my past, and break its hold over me. It would be like opening a door that I could walk through and find completeness and satisfaction. In addition to revelation from His Word, He gave me dreams in the night and a word of prophecy or visions through other people; that shed light on my problems. These occurrences are a direct result of the promise of God to pour out His Spirit on everyone that seeks him to prophesy, have dreams and see visions.[1] We don't have to remain in the darkness and muddle through our problems alone, God enables people to have supernatural insight into the hidden things, the painful memories of our lives, and He rescues us from the power of those memories. The emotional healing concerned my inner world, the way I thought about myself and other people.

I came out of active church work in Bethel Christian Centre and went to St. Mark's. The healing could not be achieved while I was busy; I needed to stand back from serving in order to see more clearly certain aspects of being engaged in church work. It was a novelty for a few weeks not to be busy in church, for I had always appeared with a keyboard under my arm and was occupied in setting it up, and being busy practising songs with the worship group. Soon, I felt like a fish out of water; I actually felt quite lost.

It was such a harrowing time. I was not going to be alone, God would be with me, but somehow I couldn't sense His Presence as strongly as before and I pined for Him. It felt like I was walking in a desert, a very dry and lonely place but I had read other people's accounts of desert experiences and so in a measure I felt comforted. I saw the challenge of the Christian life is to grow more God-centred and less self-centred; so I was willing to submit myself to this time of adjustment and healing.

i). ANOREXIA AND BULIMIA

I will share first about the eating disorder and how my thinking changed in this area. With the upsurge of the eating disorder some months after Eddy's death, I felt helpless and ashamed, but I could not stop myself from acting this way. After the first episode at age 16, I believed it was over and forgotten. But in actual fact, it occurred many times over the years, particularly after being pregnant, and at the age of 26 coping with excessive pressures, it intensified. Like an alcoholic, each time I went on a binge, I'd tell myself, "This is definitely the last time." I meant it at the time, but then when the pressure built up, I fell into the same pattern.

Two events took place that I believe triggered off the first episode. My Granny died in the Spring of '69 during my last year at school, and although I missed her very much, I was unable to express my grief. At home there was hardly any mention of her because of the hurts and tensions that had developed over the years between Granny and my parents. Granny and I had grown closer since I shared with her my newfound faith. It was at that time she discovered a living faith; committed her life to Christ and was at peace. She had softened much in her last years, and admitted to me that she had been unfair in her judgments. I was just saddened that she never spoke of this to my father.

The other difficulty was with my music, but I would never have thought to confide in anyone about it, having come up against so many barriers with adults when very young. I had been having piano lessons since I was 10 and I wanted to achieve a piano grade every year. As I mentioned before, I had aimed for two grades in one year and that's when things began to fall apart. My teacher forgot to send in the application form in time for the Grade 6 examination and I was deeply disappointed and frustrated at the postponement. It's possible that my teacher thought I wasn't ready for the exam, that I was rushing things a bit. It would take up to a year to make up for this delay. I suffered a long bout of depression, not revealing a word of my inner pain, and afterwards I went on a severe diet.

One day, during the Easter holidays, I wore a figure hugging dress which showed up all my new teenage curves, I took one look in the mirror and exclaimed in horror, "Help, I'm getting fat." I believed I was overweight, but in reality I was underweight for my height. I was determined to cut bread and potatoes down to a minimum. I was fanatical, weighing myself every day and doing floor exercises and walking. As if this wasn't enough, I bought slimming biscuits with my pocket money. The more I lost weight the better I felt. I needed to feel good about myself and so I persisted in losing weight. It was one thing I could control while other areas seemed out of control.

When a roommate discovered the slimming biscuits in my drawer I was embarrassed. I decided I wouldn't buy any more, I devised other ways of losing weight. While my classmates enjoyed pancakes and waffles in abundance for breakfast, I poked away at one measly pancake. In less than an hour I would be starving, but told myself it was good to feel the rumblings in my stomach then I knew I was losing more weight. I was completely obsessed with my weight; I would copy out mouthwatering recipes from magazines, and try them out at home when we would have visitors. I would delight in serving our visitors with generous helpings while I ate bird-sized helpings. If I couldn't get out of eating a normal portion I'd exercise all the harder, later, to burn up the calories. At night I would dream of eating delicious food. These bird-sized helpings were a carryover from my Granny. She used to chide us when we wolfed our food down quickly, and call us 'gluttons', while at the same time peeling the jackets off the potatoes and placing the potatoes on our plates to encourage us to eat. She would only eat one potato. Then another time she would tell us, "You should always leave the table with space to eat another meal." One minute she was encouraging us to eat, the next she was making us feel guilty for eating so much. These mixed messages were confusing.

I think one of the reasons why I was bothered so much

about gaining weight was the fact that my mother and my sister both had a weight problem. I saw two extremes in the home; my Granny living on "rations", and my mother and sister struggling continually with their weight. I sensed that they were both unhappy in some way and I felt very much for them. I didn't understand it; I just felt it. Granny disapproved of my mother's weight problem. It wasn't said outright, but by innuendos dropped in conversations.

It didn't help that the farming lifestyle at that time focused on big meals for the family. There was a ready supply of meat, potatoes and vegetables; most of it home grown; and the women baked homemade bread and cakes almost every day. Dinner plates were piled high with food especially potatoes. It was no wonder that many women were overweight. Granny did not go with the flow in this respect. I admired her control. She curtailed her intake of fattening foods. If anyone had an eating disorder; whether they overate or starved themselves; there was temptation in their path continually. At a family gathering, the men sometimes wanted to complement their daughters on their fine figures. These were girls that were simply well fed, that had no hang ups about diets or eating for comfort. It didn't help when the men made statements like, "There's a fine lump of a lassie"; or "There's a grand stout lassie". To them it was just admiring them, and using a phrase that was commonly used, but to an anorexic person it was unacceptable. It was said to me before I lost weight. I thought it was distasteful, and I was determined that I wouldn't grow into a "lump". It sounds so funny now; but at the time I didn't think it was funny.

Well the whole thing was getting out of hand regarding my eating disorder; when I returned home from school at the end of term looking so pale and thin my mother thought I had been ill. My weight had dropped close to seven stone. She wanted to fatten me up with lots of home cooking, but I found ways of pleasing her while still controlling my weight. Inwardly, I was growing alarmed because my whole system was undergoing unpleasant changes, it was at this time my menstrual cycle became erratic. I was afraid to tell anyone for fear they would insist I eat more food. I had to have some control in my life. In the end I was forced to confide in a friend who was a student doctor, who arranged for me to have an examination in hospital. The experience acted like a warning, it jolted me into eating more food, but I was always watchful of gaining one pound more than what I perceived was my normal weight.

I was told, very kindly, by a friend just before my first marriage, that I had a fine figure with hips that were suitable for child bearing. Women with smaller frames, she said, sometimes had difficulties giving birth. This was again the worst thing for an anorexic mind to latch on to. I imagined I had very big hips and wanted to lose weight, not thinking clearly at the time that you can lose all the weight you want to, but you can't change your bone structure.

My thought patterns were very negative. I was not happy with my appearance, or my achievements. Nobody expressed his or her real feelings at home. Since my Baptism in the Spirit the previous summer, I had returned to school where such an experience was not understood. This created further tension in me. It just seemed real issues were never addressed adequately anywhere, I was supposed to have my faith to sustain me but if nothing was ever aired how could one find out how to apply principles for life? If adults avoided awkward subjects, I was too timid to initiate a discussion. So I suffered in silence. I didn't analyse it like this at the time, I just felt I was letting God down and also my family. Eric was able to handle tensions, because he was open about everything. He had no problems with communication. My reaction was to push them down inside, it seemed a losing battle to me to try to talk about difficult issues. It just seemed too painful, caused too many disagreements.

People didn't talk about Anorexia when I was a teenager, but now there are many books on the market dealing with the subject. In my research on disorders I read a lot of these books, but the one I found the most helpful was "The Secret Language of Eating Disorders" by Peggy Claude-Pierre. She had the unbelievable heartache of two daughters suffering from Anorexia. Peggy, in seeking professional help, discovered that doctors in general and therapists believe there is no cure, and that a victim is manipulative and selfish, and tends to be a perfectionist. While I think the third point is true because of my own experience; Peggy could not accept this opinion, she writes:

"I was becoming convinced that there was an under-lying condition that predisposed people to eating disorders, not a life issue, but an interpretation of life caused by an inherent mind set."[2]

She coined the phrase, Confirmed Negativity Condition (CNC) to point out the complex way a victim's mind works. The victims hate themselves, they want to punish themselves, they feel guilty, some are afraid of public places.

Anorexia is a self-destructive behaviour, often ending in death. Fortunately for me, I was stopped in my destructive path. Victims don't analyse what they are doing, all they know is that they are unhappy with themselves and their situation and feel driven to improve themselves. They are usually intelligent, creative people, who suffer from low self-esteem, and guilt feelings about not achieving their goals. Dieting severely is a sign of an inner cry to be loved, and a cry for help but somehow they are unable to ask. They are often lonely people locked away in their negative thought patterns.

Individuals lack a sense of identity, because they focus more on pleasing people. They take the burdens of others upon themselves, worry about them, but still they think they are very uncaring. I had a tendency towards this attitude. I needed to please people. Peggy adds:

"... individuals with eating disorders have no sense of self or identity except for the fulfillment of their extremely subjective perception of other's expectations."[3]

It is a common misconception that anorexia is mainly about losing weight. It goes deeper than that; the person is usually beset with many fears. At sixteen, I was afraid to grow up, and assume the responsibilities of an adult but I could not share this with anyone for fear they would think I was stupid. I didn't know why I was afraid; the feeling was just there. Peggy suggests that anorexics shun responsibility because they have already carried burdens too heavy to bear. For myself, I worried about the tensions in my home. I worried that I couldn't attain to the standards expected of us children. Anorexia affects people to a greater or lesser degree depending on their personality. Some will suffer from mild depression while others will have deep depression, and this is exacerbated by the lack of proper nutrients. Mine was a mild form of depression, but nonetheless troublesome and I never connected the gloom that settled over me was linked to lack of proper nourishment.

Peggy Claude-Pierre opened a Clinic and organized round-the-clock supervision and support for victims of eating disorders, for she had found that an environment that provided unconditional love and positive outlook was the main thing that helped her with her own daughters. Her clinic is the only one of its kind to be successful in dealing with this killer disease.

I was very interested to find that Peggy used the term "unconditional love", for it's one thing that's very scarce in this world. Having suffered in silence myself, not knowing anyone with the same problem, or finding anyone that I knew I could trust to confide in, it was God's unconditional love that rescued me from this dreadful disease.

In my personal battle with Anorexia in adult life, it would flare up with a vengeance when I was pregnant. The truth was the reality of pregnancy depressed me. This in itself is not unnatural, for we've only to read textbooks on the subject that tell us mood swings are caused by the hormonal changes in the body. It's natural to feel emotional but what I struggled with was something far greater and subtler than hormonal changes. My anorexic inclinations clashed with the new life developing inside of me. I struggled with negative thoughts, "I look fat and ugly... why do I eat so much?"

We joke about a woman's cravings during the early months, some can long for the strangest food combinations. My craving was quite ordinary, I longed for cornflakes and bananas when I was expecting Joy. After I finished a bowl I usually felt so guilty for eating it, thinking of how fattening they were so when the hormones finally settled down, and I no longer had cravings I had a measure of control and attempted to diet so that I wouldn't gain too much weight during the pregnancy. Following the birth, I could hardly wait to diet seriously and exercise to regain my figure. The only problem was that after Joy's birth I was breastfeeding. The nurses doubted whether I had enough milk, because Joy cried a lot. I insisted that I had enough milk. The nurses tried to monitor the situation, by weighing Joy before and after each meal to see how much she was getting; but when I went home I set about dieting and exercising and so I lost too much weight.

My mother paid a surprise visit when Joy was six weeks old, and was shocked once again to find me looking thin and pale. She thought it was too much for me to breast feed, but I couldn't admit defeat. Eddy had been breast fed as an infant and was keen that I feed Joy. I was genuinely eager to bond with my baby, but I couldn't guess what an insidious force I was up against, a life threatening disorder was slowly spoiling my attempts to give my baby daughter a good start in life. A photograph was taken of the family during my Mum's visit showing how my clothes were swimming on me.

The anorexia hit big time after Eddy died. I was plagued some days with depressing thoughts like, "I don't want to talk to anyone today" or "I don't want to go out today." There was always something pressing me to hide away, to withdraw from life. I often felt devoid of feeling; nothing really moved me or excited me. But of course, after a couple of days of bingeing and starving I'd have to go outside for the sake of my children. They were my lifelines. In fact, I was no longer anorexic, my behaviour patterns had changed to bingeing and starving, according to the text books I would be described as Bulimic. I was trapped in a vicious circle.

Slowly, it began to dawn on me that my relationship with my father was related to my behaviour. All the old frustrations were coming to the surface. I remember running to him, as a child, in the front field as he walked up the hill to count the cattle. I wanted to tell him so much of the things I had been doing, for example, a game I had been playing with my brother, Isaac, in the woods. Dad could be surprisingly funny sometimes, humming a tune or making up a rhyme. But he was not in the mood for making up rhymes this particular day. Instead, I heard him muttering under his breath. I greeted him enthusiastically, hoping to cheer him up. He seemed to be scolding some unfortunate person as if they were right in front of him and his voice was growing louder and louder. I asked him who he was talking to, and that was my mistake. He told me not to bother him, and continued to scold the invisible offender. I tried to get his attention again, but he completely ignored me, he just walked faster and scolded some more. I turned around, disconsolately, and went home.

Sometimes this quirk of Dad's could be quite funny, like the stormy evening we were sitting in the study with Granny and we heard voices outside the window. "Helen, go and call your Dad." Granny ordered. "Tell him to bring his visitor inside. There's a good fire burning here." I went off outside reluctantly and called Dad; it was cold and dark and I stood at the corner of the house near the front door, and listened. I thought Dad was standing nearby, because I could hear him quite clearly; but then I realised that he was standing at the other end of the house, and the wind was carrying the sound of his voice closer to me. He seemed to be arguing with someone; he was giving them a proper grilling but soon I realised there was no one with him. When I called him again, he was furious and told me to go inside.

Granny was highly amused when she heard Dad was alone. "What's he so annoyed about, serves him right if he catches a cold." And she dismissed the whole thing, laughing at the comical side, having first thought that Dad was talking to a neighbour; so we laughed along with her, it was our way of coping with tension. She teased Dad when he finally came in for supper, but he ignored her and sat in a huff while he ate.

It Happened Again

When Dad was in this kind of mood no one could reason with him. It seemed he was locked into a certain mind frame and no remonstrating could shake him out of it. I think this was Dad's way of airing his feelings, he wanted to be on his own to think aloud, but, as in any family, little people tend to intrude. Dad couldn't cope with our interruptions; he was so often preoccupied with his thoughts.

Another frustrating time was when we'd go to give him a hug at bedtime. Usually he was eating his supper and he'd hold us off with a grumpy response, or allow us give him a quick peck on the cheek, then say, "Off with you, off with you." He was so unapproachable. I would hunger for his affection, and when he waved us away it hurt so much. Mum would allow us to kiss her but she was a bit reserved when it came to cuddles and I would climb the stairs to bed feeling bereft and build daydreams of parents that were more affectionate. My dream world was very real to me, compensating for the lack of attention.

I read somewhere that little girls need affirmation from their father especially, otherwise they feel incomplete, and they develop low self-esteem if it is neglected. I longed for his affirmation, his praise and approval regarding things and activities I was involved in, for example, when I went to show him a new dress I was wearing. This was my very own dress, chosen by me, not a cast-off from my sisters, as was often the case. It was very important to me that he take notice of me in that special dress then I could hold my head high knowing that my father had showed an interest in me. But no, he couldn't stop reading the newspaper long enough to take a really good look, and offer an unconditional word of praise, instead it came out as an impatient response that made me feel embarrassed and wished that

I had never asked him to share the moment with me. It's an awful thing to say, but it felt like he didn't really sit up and take notice of me until tragedy almost wrecked my life.

As I grew older, I picked up the reasons for my father's tension and anger. It seemed that no matter what he did to please his mother, it never worked. He tried to come up to her expectations, and they were pretty high expectations, and so he lived under a cloud of disapproval. He felt he had failed. His way of coping was to take off when things proved too much for him and spend the day in the pubs. This annoyed my mother intensely, especially if she expected him home with some shopping. It annoyed us children if we happened to be with him in the village and we were waiting in the car for him to come out. At first, we would hardly notice that he was late coming, because we would be eating lollipops or bags of penny sweets. But when we'd get through eating time would drag, then we'd discuss whether we'd face going into the pub after him, or just walk home. We tried a few times to get him out, but it was so embarrassing that we usually opted for walking home.

I couldn't understand why there should be tension between Dad and his mother. Why didn't they talk it over like sensible human beings and sort everything out? I loved them both and wanted so much that they get on well together. I respected my Granny very much. She was a very frail woman, physically, but had great strength of character. She was a formidable person with very high standards, and expected us all to tow the line.

She was the sort of person I could imagine living in a great mansion in the Victorian era, having regular visitors for afternoon teas with delicate cucumber sandwiches and scones. When people were invited to our home, she would have Mum in a flap with her high standards of etiquette and social behaviour, and warnings to us to behave ourselves, not to speak unless spoken to, not to speak with our mouths full etc.! We would be exasperated with all the rules and preferred to stay out in the kitchen and wolf our way through tiny ham sandwiches and cakes, or better still snatch a handful of sandwiches before Mum cut the crusts off and take them out to our hide-out in the woods!

To give her credit, Granny influenced me greatly in having regular devotions when she read the Bible and prayed. During my holidays she would ask me to share in her quiet time, and because I was curious about the characters and events in the Bible I would join her. It was often a matter of rule or form, but it set a precedent for my life. Devotions became more interesting in my teens after my conversion. Often during these quiet times, I would long for the prayers to end, so I could chat with her about her childhood. She told me I was her favourite grandchild because I sat and talked with her. At those times, it was just me and her, I felt very close to her and I wished that the rest of our family life was as good as this.

But then, something would happen to spoil it all. It didn't take much to set Granny off. If I ran upstairs two or three steps at a time, she would shout at me because it wasn't lady-like, or if I whistled loudly while I dusted the ornaments in her bedroom. She used to quote this saying: "A whistling woman and a crowing hen, there's no luck in the house therein." It seemed such a funny thought, but she said it in such a disapproving manner that would make me check the rising laughter. How quickly the atmosphere changed if I dared answer back and say that it wasn't such a big deal to do such things.

Some rooms were off limits to us children. We were not allowed into the sitting room, (except to practise the piano) or the spare bedroom, they were kept for visitors. Of course the very fact that we were told not to go into these rooms made us want to go all the more. And so we sneaked in quietly and played some game. It was the adherence to religious duty and family expectation along with Granny controlling the household that wore my father down, and affected us children a great deal. Things were often emphasized in anger, when all we wanted was a soft word and the reassurance that we were loved, no matter what we did or didn't achieve.

I discovered that Dad's drinking binges and my eating binges were similar in the sense that we were two people ill at ease with our inner selves. This made us dependent on certain behaviour patterns. We struggled terribly with guilt feelings and perfectionism. We had unreasonable standards to uphold.

This point helped me to understand my own make-up and it surprised me to find it was similar to my father's. The point about perfectionism stayed with me. "Was I really a perfectionist?" A perfectionist sounded like someone that fussed a lot about things, was hard to please, like my Granny when I dusted her bedroom. Was I a fussy person, I asked myself? We called Granny a "fusspot," because she irritated us so much with her finicky ways. As I thought about it I could see I was following the same pattern.

To illustrate how disappointed and impatient I could get when things were not perfect, I will share about the episode of the Swiss roll. It was my first time to try baking one. I was fuming when I couldn't get it out of the tin in one piece. I felt it mocked me as I looked at the miserable effort sitting, broken, on the wire tray. I couldn't bear to look at it; I had to get rid of it. I was married to Eddy at the time, and he heard me express my dismay and tried to cheer me up. "It's not so bad." He laughed infuriating me. I can laugh about it now, but I was deadly serious then. He went out of the kitchen momentarily, and I flung the cake in the dustbin. When he returned, he looked around. "Where is it?" he asked. I pointed to the dustbin. He couldn't believe it. "I was looking forward to a piece of that," he said," I didn't mind that it was broken. The birds would even have enjoyed the crumbs." And he reached into the dustbin to get some cake for the birds. My attitude was, OUT OF SIGHT, OUT OF MIND. I didn't want to be reminded of it by coming across scraps of cake in the garden later on. If I could have dealt the same way with the music failure, it would have been so easy!

Reading the Bible kept me sane, I resorted to it for it stated: "The Lord is a refuge for the oppressed..."[4] I had no solution so I just kept reading the Bible, at least it relieved the darkness of my depression. I began to change my outlook when I was studying the bi-monthly devotional "Every Day with Jesus" - Selections from the Psalms- (23rd Psalm) - by Selwyn Hughes. One morning I read:

"The basic spiritual and physical needs of men and women...are threefold:

(1) The need to feel secure

(2) The need to feel significant and

(3) The need to feel a sense of self-worth.

If these needs are not met then we experience the opposite of these three words, namely, insecurity, insignificance, and inferiority."[5]

Selwyn Hughes believed the Good Shepherd longs that we find out for ourselves the safety of His love, the importance of His plan for our lives and the esteem He holds for each one of us, as we walk in the rich pastures of His Word. In building up my self-esteem, I read much the following verses: "O Lord...You know me...You are familiar with all my ways."[6] "Many...are the things You planned for us."[7] We are in God's thoughts. A sense of security began to develop as these words became personal to me: "Fear not, for I have redeemed you, I have summoned you by name; you are mine."[8] "Who are kept by the power of God through faith."[9] In my longing for significance and achievement, I dwelled much on this verse: "The Lord will fulfil His purpose for me: Your love endures forever."[10] These verses made me feel good about myself.

When Christ put His finger on this problem by consistent teaching from His Word, I received strength to adjust my behaviour patterns. It was something I had to continually watch and work at, but my weight grew steadier. It took time for me to accept the given weight for my height.

At this time I was also able to take the step of forgiving my father and grandmother for the impossible standards they expected us to live up to without a murmur, it was time to stop blaming them for the past and to take responsibility for my own actions. Forgiveness does not come easily to us, it is alien to our nature, but as we all stand in need of God's forgiveness, it is necessary to show forgiveness to others. There is an old proverb that goes like this: "He who cannot forgive others breaks the bridge over which he himself must pass." Unforgiveness is actually harmful, some doctors say it can be the cause of many illnesses, such as cancer and arthritis. As it eats away on the inside of a person it begins to show in their physical body. In my own case, to forgive my father, especially, for the past was like shedding a great weight. I needed to forgive my father and grandmother, and to obtain a release from generational ties, the control that Granny held over us.

It's funny how our perception of people associated with us, and events in our lives cause us to have a distorted view. It's like looking at life through a filter, so that the picture we have of life is not necessarily the true picture. It is how we perceive them as the result of unhappy experiences.

Talking to Joan, my sister, around the time of writing this, she agreed with me that our perceptions are not always accurate. We wanted our parents to give us a word of praise, but they never did in the way we expected. She clarified this by telling me that Mum and Dad didn't praise us to our face, it was the era we were brought up in. Parents didn't praise or affirm their children for fear they'd get bigheaded. They gave praise in an indirect way. Dad would praise Joan, for instance, to me and then another occasion would talk with Joan and say good things about me. When we left home and had families of our own, Mum would write long letters to Joan in Canada all about Margaret, Isaac and myself; and Mum would write to me and tell me with pride the events in Joan, Margaret and Isaac's lives.

Our Aunties did exactly the same when we were younger, Joan felt for a long time that it seemed all she heard was stuff about me, she wanted to know something about herself for a change. Didn't they have any praise left for her? "Helen is very talented, she can play the piano like Aunty Mabel, she'll go far" or an Aunt would comment, "Helen has good looks, just like her Aunty Mabel."

I remember Mum and Dad both praising Joan a lot about what a wonderful baby she was, especially when she was learning to talk, how she could wrap Dad around her little finger. Dad seemed to glow about his firstborn child and Margaret and I just seemed to pale into insignificance. Isaac was also doted over because he was the son and heir. Aunty Kathleen too, would talk endlessly about Joan's talent for sparkling conversation and other talents and so it went on. Dad did comment, "I'm not worried about Helen, she has the looks, she'll marry for sure. But I'll have to buy husbands for Joan and Margaret." On this occasion he was joking.

When Joan told me all this stuff my reaction was "I wish they had told me at the time. It would have meant so much to me. "Still, it shows our parents did care about us, in their own way, and followed events in our lives with interest. It's just unfortunate that because we didn't perceive it that way, we developed certain behaviours to compensate. Some children can get cocky, and try to prove to their parents they can succeed, trying hard to win their approval, achieving a measure of success in their chosen subject. Other children allow people to put them down. I was like that, developing low self-esteem and facing failure. I longed continually for my father's approval, when I didn't get it I turned anorexic. It was a question of perception, and now that I understood it to a certain extent I felt much better.

While all this helped me greatly and brought my eating disorder under control; it didn't completely set my mind and heart at ease. I had gained help from Christian psychologists but it only renewed my conscious mind. I still hurt inside. Although the conscious mind had been renewed, sadly, as with many people, the subconscious was not renewed. Occasionally, when I heard references being made to the hang-ups in adults because of the damage done in childhood, I would be surprised at the disquiet within me while I heard these things being discussed. Then I would dismiss it, thinking that I had dealt enough with this; it was time to move on.

Yet I couldn't move on, even though I tried very hard. People pressed my buttons in certain situations and I could feel tension rising up within me and I'd find myself arguing with them. Usually there was no resolution, only unease.

Years passed and one weekend I attended a Conference in Castlewellan, Co. Down where Keith Gerner spoke on The Orphan Spirit. At one point he mentioned that people have a need for fathering; where their father didn't affirm them or give them unconditional love as a child. They will need healing in their emotions. This touched a chord in me. I knew Dr. Don Woods was present at the Conference and was scheduled to speak on Theophostics in the afternoon. I decided to ask him, as soon as possible, for a consultation. He agreed and slotted me in immediately after his talk.

I will just explain, briefly, that Theophostics is a form of inner healing. The word originated with Dr. Edward Smith. It is taken from the greek word, theos (God) and phos (light) and the form of healing ministry that he developed: In simple terms, it is assisting people to experience the light of God's Word dispelling the darkness and lies that have developed in their minds during childhood as a result of hurtful experiences; these experiences are stored in the subconscious and current experiences, often only vaguely related to them, will evoke painful emotions.

During the consultation with Don Woods I told him that this friend of mine would press my buttons in a discussion and tension would build up within me most times. This friend didn't seem to be listening to what I was saying; he would cut me short. Don asked me if I could remember a similar situation in childhood. I could remember my father doing this frequently; and I felt it stemmed from the fact that, to Dad, I was just another girl. I heard it related often enough, that Dad was disappointed when I was born. He wanted a son and heir. I was his third daughter, just another girl. I just felt that he never had any time for me. Don asked me how I felt when this occurred, I replied that I felt unwanted, unloved, that I didn't deserve attention. Don paused a moment and prayed, "Lord, what do You say about this?" He waited a moment; I could hear the words of Jesus in my mind, "I've got all the time in the world for you." I repeated the words with joy and certainty. Immediately the truth of these words broke the lie that I had believed for years. I started to laugh at the immense relief that welled up inside of me replacing the inner tension and strain.

Once I had been healed, I found that memories long forgotten, of my father's care, came to mind. One particular incident took place when I was about three years old. It was a Sunday and we had just sat down to dinner when Dad asked one of us to put away his prayer book in the cupboard beside the fire. Margaret and I made a dash for the book, and I tumbled into the hearth burning part of my left arm. My memory is a blur here; people were rushing to get antiseptic creams and trying to soothe me. When my screams subsided and I was exhausted Mum took me upstairs to bed. It was some hours later, I woke at dusk, to find Dad at my bedside, looking down at me, his blue eyes full of concern. He asked me if I wanted to get up, and when I nodded he lifted me gently from the bed and carried me downstairs. He couldn't do enough for me, because I had got injured while doing something for him. I treasure this memory of my father, and I know better now that he did try to look after us in the best way he knew at that time. I think I misunderstood my father greatly; in those days, most fathers focused very much on providing for their families, they didn't think much about the emotional side of things.

It was the same with Granny, I cherish the memory of my

last conversation with her. As I went to say goodbye, before I returned to boarding school, I was very struck with her fragile appearance. She was about 82 years old and had suffered a number of falls and her voice was growing weaker, I sensed she would not be with us for very long. I had an urge to linger with her and was prompted to suggest we pray together. When I had finished my prayer Granny asked if I would read the 23rd Psalm; as I started to read she spoke some of the words along with me. As we uttered those comforting, unchanging words we were drawn into the warm embrace of the Father's arms. It was a tangible sensation and it strengthened us to make our goodbyes. As I turned to go, she told me to fetch her handbag from the wardrobe, she wanted to give me a red ten-shilling note for pocket money. It was exactly a week later that my uncle came to take me home from school; Granny had died from a heart attack early that morning. For a long time I had forgotten this precious time with Granny, instead, whenever I thought of her funeral all I could see was the stony face of my father as he struggled with his memories of her. Now they are both in heaven, for Dad too finally found his peace before his death, and I am confident that they enjoy one another's company in a way they never knew while on earth.

ii). COMMUNICATION

I believe my eating disorder was the result of low self-esteem. I had very little sense of self because I sought to please others and live up to the expectations of others. This affected my communication with people and how I approached God. This was the second area in which I experienced healing. It's very early in life, that the way we handle life's experiences ultimately dictates how we handle things later in life. We build up a pattern of behaviour in these early days. Our environment in which we are nurtured is firstly the home, our interactions with family then our experience and interaction with staff and pupils at school. It's all about how we handle perceived challenges to our self-esteem and security, which determine our behaviour in later life.

I longed to communicate with people but couldn't get passed surface chat. I was very shy at this time and found it extremely difficult to hold a conversation. I didn't know how to get to a deeper level with folk. I guess it was because I was unable to open up about my real feelings. If I took the risk of sharing how I really felt I would be exposing my insecurities. I had an inkling that I wasn't being real about myself to others when I heard Eric observe about a certain individual: "He's not being real." I began to see that there are different levels of communication.

I asked myself the question, if I am not being real, how does this manifest itself? It occurred when I didn't discuss my real feelings, then I was, in effect, pretending, putting on a mask. It became apparent that I was ignoring my problems, pushing them down inside, and acting as if they didn't exist.

When I came to communicate with God; I would pray and think that everything was all right when it wasn't; I was deceiving myself. While I thought there was nothing amiss then God couldn't communicate with me or do anything to help because I wasn't being real about my need. I found that He preferred that I pour out my heartfelt need to Him; then He could interact with me and offer solutions to my problems.

It was an eye-opener, to think that I was wearing a mask. Trying hard to please God with my distorted thinking, not as the Word of God stated. This was the key to my locked emotions. I had tried so hard to converse with God and man but could not get much beyond the surface level. To reach a deeper level depended on my opening up to another about my choices and feelings but I could not get beyond this point for many years, for I was so focused on the other person while I was with them. At the back of my mind was the thought: "They couldn't possibly be interested in my opinions."

I realised there's got to be real trust and a willingness to reveal my inner self in order to build up relationships with others; but if I was bent on relating without total openness and honesty those relationships would break down. It is too easy to read into what is said, or to feel threatened, or to feel I will burden the other person. This was how I felt about relationships in the past. Now I saw it was important to express clearly what I wanted to say then there would be no room for misunderstanding. I may not get it right the first or second time because I'm in a learning process but it is vital for me to connect with reality in open communication.

If feelings are not expressed, then they are pushed down, and long term this can cause untold damage. We are thrown off balance, and develop prejudices and complexes. It's not possible to keep in contact with our real self.

Very slowly, I began to talk in real terms. I was learning that God likes to show affection and to lavish His love upon us. I had been so set on trying to impress Him, to be on my best behaviour, that it robbed me of all the joy of knowing Him. The way forward was to rely on His free grace, and let go of doing it my way. I believe my view of my father affected my view of God; in the sense that I had difficulty relating to Dad, always feeling I had to seek his approval. So I felt it was the same with God that I would have to win his approval.

When I was finally able to open up to God, His love flowed into my life like rivers. My heart rejoiced; my step quickened. Now communication with God was stimulating and challenging. I looked forward to meeting with Him each morning and getting better acquainted. It was like a honeymoon period. I read these inviting words: "I have loved you with an everlasting love; I have drawn you with loving-kindness".[11] I understood that this love would always exist, it was not like the sugary love that is portrayed on T.V and in magazines; it is not a love that ebbs and flows, but a love that is strong and true, always constant.

He prompted me to waken early in the morning to listen carefully to His instruction.[12] He taught me that His acceptance of me was not based on my performance, not on my prayers, my church attendance, my work, but simply because He loved me through the new covenant He has made. He was committed to me because of his sacrifice on Calvary. My sins were forgiven, nothing stood in the way of communion with him. This was something joyous, and very precious.

There was something about His mercy and love that drew me to Him; I read that God has an abundance of mercy and compassion; there is no limit to His supply.[13] It was this that helped me communicate with Him. I didn't have to hide my failings from Him; He loved me despite them. It was like I had discovered a vast storehouse filled with mercy and love, and there was no sign of it running out.

I was getting a picture of a deep, committed love, not easily given and then snatched back. How can I express what this meant to me? All I can do is try to convey how the Holy Spirit took my meditation and just seemed to make me so aware of God's mercy that He wanted to pour out generously upon me.

It Happened Again

It seemed that the walls of my bedroom receded, and I was standing in 'God's house' completely taken up with him and He was lavishly bestowing mercy upon mercy upon me, like someone giving me presents every day. I saw that I could have as much of God as I wanted.

My diary, at this time, is full of my delight in God each morning as I meditated upon Him. There were no barriers like before, there was no guilt, I was given dreams in the night showing me my sins were cleansed. One night, I dreamt I was in the dock of a courtroom, and my accuser was throwing all sorts of accusations at me. It was terrifying to witness his wrath, and his mocking me. But the judge took no notice of him, and completely pardoned me. The sense of relief was exquisite.

This set me free to improve my communication with my fellow man. I put my foot in it many times as I slowly began to reveal my true self. It was better to make mistakes than to endure further frustration. I will include how a start was made to deal with the frustration and anger within me in this section, for anger can sometimes be a destructive form of communication.

I attended a Ladies Breakfast meeting in St. Mark's one Easter. One of the speakers asked us to make a commitment to be our children's keeper. This was more than praying regularly for them; she was asking us to go further and do spiritual warfare on their behalf. This meant to actually fight for them because there are so many pressures our children are faced with that mothers need to roll up their sleeves, as it were, and get into battle for their youngsters. Not just allow things to happen, and say, "well, it's the times we live in; and we should let our children make up their own minds." I agree that we have to give them the freedom to make choices but we can help them behind the scenes to make wise choices. A mother who joins ranks with the Almighty on behalf of her child is a force to be reckoned with! She can make her arch enemy cringe and fall back for daring to interfere with her child.

This opened up a floodgate of emotions for me as I thought of the confrontations I had had with my girls, especially Joy, I got so angry and it grieved me. I felt defeated and frustrated. I had been approaching Joy in defeat. I didn't always appreciate, at the time, that a lot of Joy's daring to resist discipline and daring to rebel was her way of dealing with the loss of her father. She protested more loudly than the others. I decided that I needed to be more positive, and not to speak on the defensive or with a tone of defeat. I addressed all the anger and frustration. It was a time of healing and restoration. There was a marked improvement in our family life from this point in being real and communicating more effectively. It didn't mean that we never got angry again, but that where I lashed out verbally and unreasonably before, or retreated in denial, now I faced an issue or at least made an effort to face it.

I still had to face a point with both Esther and Joy in their late teens, when they needed healing from the way they had slipped into trying to protect me from difficulties. There was a great need for open communication here. Because they had picked up how I would react so strongly to their misbehaviour, and they knew I was now the sole parent with much responsibility, they tried to spare me trouble. It caused them to grow up prematurely, but emotionally they couldn't handle the burden. Esther, in her quiet way, would try to shoulder some of the burden, and talk to her sisters and get them to behave. When Esther left home, Joy took on this role with Eleanor but because it was an unnatural role it caused much grief. There were arguments and name calling between them. Other times, Joy being sensitive to my mood, (she is very like me, a very sensitive intense person, it is not surprising that we clashed) adopted a sort of counselling role with me, coming home from college with ideas she had picked up there. We went through a very bad period then, it got very complicated because when there are three emotional females all trying to uphold their side of the argument there were sparks flying. We were in need of a neutral person to bring perspective. While trying to speak out our differences we were making a big mess of it. It got that we couldn't talk without getting upset. We just wanted to get well away from each other. Joy with the eagerness and openness of youth wanted it all cleared up one night. But we were going around in circles. I was unable to find perspective as quickly as she wanted. It was at this point I drew back from Joy. I left Joy so we could both cool down overnight and went to a friend's house to discuss it in confidence.

While Joy and I had time to reflect, we tried to understand the other person's point of view. Joy sought help from a counsellor. One night I had the idea to write a letter to Joy, as we couldn't talk easily together. I wrote down where I saw we both had exceeded the boundaries in our relationship. Joy accepted the letter, but told me she didn't want a discussion immediately. She needed time to think. I had to be patient and wait. All was silent for about a month, Joy appearing occasionally for Sunday dinner where we kept the topics simple. Then at church one night we received some insight.

One of the leaders had a vision where she saw two pieces of a puzzle interlocking, she sensed the meaning was two members of a family affected by disunity, would come together. It would not happen by our efforts, but by the power of God's

Spirit.[14] Intuitively, I just knew this referred to the misunderstanding between Joy and I. Later, I found that Joy also felt the same about the vision. We were torn by strife and misunderstanding, and now we were greatly encouraged by this promise that we would be reunited. Very slowly, bit-by-bit, the pieces of the puzzle came together. We saw where we had both made mistakes and our relationship began to mend.

Even with this encouraging vision, Joy and I kept our distance. It was a delicate situation and needed to be handled carefully, or the rift would never be healed. Joy had a hard time believing that I was willing to keep within the boundaries that I had stated during this painful period. I experienced such a softening and spirit of forgiveness that I was able to reach out to Joy in an unconditional way. I felt such tenderness well up in me towards her. Joy had always looked for a lot of attention from me, the demand used to overwhelm me because of my past. Now, I was enabled to cross the barriers and bestow an expansive love on her.

I think Joy found the change in me too good to be true, but as the months went on and it only got better between us she relaxed with me, and now our relationship is stronger than ever. When I asked Joy for her permission to share this difficult period, she admitted that she frequently provoked me; and is aware that this is something she has to watch in her relationships with family and friends.

iii). ORPHAN SPIRIT

I touched on the Orphan spirit in the section on Anorexia; but there was another layer of hurt that was removed in 1993 while attending Bethel Christian Centre. One day the pastor's wife, Pauline, asked me if there was something connected to my past that needed attention. She told me the thought 'boarding school' had come to her and she felt it had something to do with me. I couldn't think of anything at that point.

I thought no more of it until a few weeks later, when I had a vivid dream one night. I was back in Drewstown, I saw myself walk into my dormitory and stand by my bed. To my surprise, there was a baby lying in the bed. I reached for the baby, and found it's nappy was wet. I took the baby downstairs and went looking for a staff member to give me some nappies. I couldn't find any assistance.

The dream remained clear in my mind after waking; I was so struck by the baby's urgent need and my inability to meet the need in the dream. I thought there was some message in the dream, and asked God to give me the interpretation. God had begun to speak to me in my dreams. I was so excited at first that I read into every one of them. I quickly learned that not all dreams come from God; I had to use discernment. I believed that God held the interpretation to my dream. I sensed this dream was important. This is what came to me: the baby was one part of my personality that had not developed during childhood and was further complicated by being sent to boarding school. It was my emotional side that had been sadly neglected. I developed an orphan spirit at this time. Without father or mother at a crucial time, facing adolescence.

I was shocked at the revelation yet I knew it was true, deep down inside of me. I wept at the memories it evoked. I had dreaded being sent away to boarding school at the age of 12 years. I didn't know how I could cope without seeing my mother regularly, and knowing her care. I missed so much the freedom of our spacious home, the fields, the beauty of the countryside. To be placed in a dull, grey institution type building in

Emotional Healing

the centre of a town, felt like prison to me. Here we were only allowed out of school on Saturdays for an hour to spend our pocket money; and only allowed visits home two Sundays in one term, and one long weekend at half term. The distance from my home was about 15 miles but I might as well have been a thousand miles away. The restrictions and loss wounded my spirit. I was not ready, emotionally, to leave home and the wrenching was agonizing.

I made no loud objections, having been conditioned long before, not to create a fuss. No one would listen. I wept at night for weeks before I went, while my mother spent days buying my school uniform and sewing on name tabs on every item of clothing. My heart would tighten with physical pain every time I ran into the kitchen and saw the large suitcase filling up with all those new school clothes. On the day I was to leave home, my brother, Isaac, ran out into the woods and wept his heart out. He and I had been inseparable and now his playmate was going away. He told me this much later, he wondered how it was I didn't cry. He didn't know how I had learned to stifle my tears because no one would listen. I had begged my mother once before; when very small; not to leave me some place I didn't want to be and she wouldn't listen. I think in some cases, parents can get so fixed on their own plan for their child that they overlook some pressing need. It wasn't urgent that I should be in that place. Anyway, once I went to school I continued to pine for home.

Some teenagers took to boarding school like ducks to water. They seemed to have no trouble adjusting; they just got on with their studies and thrived. Others suffered migraine headaches, bed-wetting or ran away. The one thing that compensated for me in this setting was my piano practise. I loved music, and ever

It Happened Again

since I watched Aunty Mabel play the piano at home I longed to be able to play. At boarding school we were allowed about twenty minutes to practise. This was my time alone, and the music soothed my inner turmoil. I loved the opportunity to stay longer, if someone missed his or her practise time. When I finished my own work, then I'd try pieces in someone else's book.

The orphan feeling continued through the second year away from home although Mum had taken Joan and I away from the boarding school. Dad had been paying fees for three daughters and was complaining about the expense. He didn't see the point in sending us to school. He thought we would marry farmers one day, why did we need an education?! Mum insisted on giving us an education, for which we are all very thankful. So instead of the boarding school, we were sent to stay with Mum's eldest sister while we attended the convent in her nearest town. I don't know why we couldn't have gone to our local convent and cycled home each day. I can't quite remember how the arrangement came about; I just have some recollection of Uncle Jimmy, Mum's brother, having a hand in it.

It didn't really work out, we were an added responsibility for Aunt Frances who suffered with Arthritis. My Aunt did her best for us, but it wasn't home. Again, it was music that saved the day. Aunt Frances didn't have a piano, but when the nuns heard I liked the piano and had nowhere to practise, I was given permission to practise on the piano in our classroom during lunch hour. This turned out to be far more stimulating that any music lessons. Another girl who played the piano used to join me and we learned duets and waltzes together. The classroom rang with noise and laughter. The result of this was the headmistress asking us to play together during a school concert at the end of the year.

Emotional Healing

Finally, Mum found Drewstown. It was a great improvement on the first boarding school, as I've mentioned already, there were lots of trees and green fields surrounding the house. However even with all the physical and spiritual advantages of this latest school, I needed mothering and because the link was broken off at the tender age of 12 with my mother, I could not communicate with her adequately in my mid-teens.

I could not communicate with the school staff. I needed their help but was unable to communicate because of my hang-ups. I did not trust people enough to share my inner hurt. I didn't even think I was hurt. People had failed me when I was little, at the time when I needed them to listen to me. I had no idea at the age of 14, while I was in Drewstown what my need was, I was so accustomed to repressing my feelings. The problem at the time was the long bout of depression that I mentioned following Granny's death. It came up some years later in conversation with Eric; he told me that the headmistress, who he found very approachable, had said to him at the time of the depression or soon after, that she was concerned about my state of mind and if I had remained much longer in it she would have interfered. I also heard from another source that she prayed for her pupils and I realise now that she must have prayed for me then. I hadn't been aware that the situation was being monitored because I was too depressed at the time.

Now, with the insight received from this dream, it was time to put this right. These words came into my mind. "But unto you that fear my name shall the Sun of righteousness arise with healing in his wings."[15] I found, on reading the context, that there were extra words. "And ye shall go forth and grow up as calves of the stall." I saw that these words indicated a healthy growth like well fed calves; not scrawny or malnourished.

This passage came to me, almost like a prophetic word, a promise of liberty and full restitution. God was promising to heal me, where I had been emotionally deprived as a child. Finally, another verse gave a lot of comfort. "I will not leave you as orphans; I will come to you."[16] I became aware of the father heart of God. Often, I would repeat the words as I quietly meditated, and they entered the forlorn area of my life, putting to rights the lack of parental care at a very vulnerable age.

iv). REPRESSED GRIEF

The fourth area of healing focused on my grief. Death had robbed me of my partners, and left me reeling physically and emotionally. Part of me had died with my husbands; I couldn't talk about this area of my life. I couldn't cry, the tears were locked deep inside. It was like I was bound in grave clothes but as I went through the process of healing, gradually the grave clothes were being removed. Some of my friends and church leaders said there wasn't any grief work to deal with; they were reluctant to touch the past. They thought I was coping well enough. They didn't know the area in my life that was hidden so well. I hardly knew, until the Lord shone his spotlight over it. I was uncomfortable with an emotional issue like this. Slowly I understood the defence mechanisms I had used to survive. I want to share the process, for it was very real and has had a lasting effect on me.

I think a part of me was shrouded in grief, it affected me so deeply that my emotions were dulled, both joys and grief's, in daily life. Because I suppressed my feelings I often thought I was indifferent to my own situation and anyone else's I came into contact with. The other part of me kept going, determined to be brave, to be faithful to God. I thought I should uphold

Christian attitudes even praising God regularly, being positive.

This activity is very uplifting as long as it is a genuine two-way exchange between God and man. If a person is simply going through the motions it is not very productive. I think Christians can fool themselves a lot of the time, having gone through this myself. It's possible to live in denial, while outwardly you seem all right. You're doing all the right things. But inside, your world has been shaken through some shattering event and you are struggling for understanding and support to carry you through. The support, the knowledge of God that you experienced up to the day of that event doesn't seem to reach far enough to cover you now. And so you develop a way of behaviour to cope. For some people their behaviour is acceptable enough so as not to draw too much attention to their problem. For others their problem is very obvious. I was in the first category and for a number of years after the initial bereavement it was satisfactory enough. In the praise times at church I meant what I said, it was better for me to be there in my wounded state than not at all.

In time the frustrations built up and I wasn't really progressing in the various activities I was engaged in. I would really be getting places, so it seemed for a time, and then, wham...I'd fall flat on my face. These periods were what I called mini-breakdowns. They would happen behind closed doors, no one else saw them. I guess the children felt more the effects of them, my mood swings, tension in the air, that sort of thing. I always came up against some barrier within myself, I didn't know what exactly. Then I'd go to church where some hymn or sermon would give me hope, or I'd read some book where a paragraph would jump out at me and I would sense God's compassion. He would lift me up again (maybe He was trying to get me to see a way out of this, but I missed it every time). I would go for weeks or months almost on a high until I faced the barrier again. I guess there came a day when God said, "Enough." He wanted the pattern broken.

I had developed a mechanism. I would act a certain way to hide my grief. In fact, it was pushed down so far I didn't know it was there. Gradually, I noticed my behaviour. Not once did I cry since the first day I heard the awful news of my husbands' deaths. I wouldn't mention the subject willingly, it was only as people enquired or touched on it. But there would be a lump in my throat, and a dull ache inside, as if I wanted to cry, but couldn't. I had learned to brace myself not to give way. Occasionally I would talk to the children about their fathers usually to mention the anniversary of their death or birthday, or a memory would be triggered off by some event. There were no photographs of Eric or Eddy about the place. Just for a little while after Eddy's death, I kept two framed photos in my bedroom, but for some reason I took them down. I guess I couldn't bear to look at them, but wouldn't admit it to myself. It was a tightly controlled situation. I had grown accustomed to the mechanism; the mask of denial was firmly in place. It was during the period of healing that I began to display them once again.

There was a wound deep in my spirit. Outwardly I was brave, but inside the wound festered away. Talking of being brave cropped up in a conversation with a friend, who pointed out; "God is close to the broken heart not the brave heart."[17] The brave heart is too self-contained. I also observed that I couldn't maintain the anointing in my life, the sense of the Presence of God. I know, that we of ourselves cannot maintain it. It is something that develops between the Holy Spirit and an individual when there are no barriers.

It frustrated me, in the area of service, for example, involved in a worship group. The Holy Spirit usually gives an anointing or empowering to enable and carry one through a given task. As I pressed into God to know him better it grew in intensity. It would almost bowl me over; it was so powerful. But then some weeks it seemed to leak away, and I was left feeling bereft and powerless in the middle of a service.

Now I'm aware there are reasons for the anointing to be absent. A person could be over-tired or trying too hard, or personal sin is blocking the anointing. I was the sort of person, brought up in the great evangelical tradition, to diligently examine myself and confess my sin regularly. In fact, like most evangelicals, I was over diligent, over conscientious. So having examined my heart I knew it wasn't sin in my life. Therefore, I was astonished to hear a pastor share a word of wisdom, comparing a wounded person to a bucket with holes; the bucket can't hold the anointing. It described my frustration accurately. My spirit leaked because of the deep-rooted wound within it. It didn't just date back to the double tragedy, but to an earlier date when feelings were disregarded and swept under the carpet.

I started to remove the mask with God; gradually I began to express the terrible pain I'd felt over Eric and Eddy's loss. But something buried so deeply took some time to rise to the surface. While it was rising, I experienced a terrible darkness and emptiness, like a separation from God. There's a saying, "It's always darkest before dawn." I didn't know that deliverance was just around the corner. I couldn't pray; nothing made sense. Then thoughts of suicide disturbed me. A voice in my head would taunt me while driving the car, "It would be so easy to kill yourself. Why don't you do it? Everything's getting on top of you." It took a tremendous effort to fight back. I would say,

"No, no, I wouldn't do this to my children, they've suffered enough." I thought of a widow friend who succumbed to these kinds of thoughts, when everything got too much for her, she took her own life.

During this time, my mother was suffering from Alzheimer's and resident in a nursing home. I was heartbroken, standing helplessly by, while she retreated into a silent world. Mum and I had reached a new level of communication as I became more real about my feelings and we would share our devotions sometimes and discuss spiritual topics. Therefore it was all the more heart rending now that she was slipping away from me. I realised just how much she had been there for me. I remember blurting out to my pastor's wife, "I need a mother". The pressure was becoming so unbearable; I felt so broken inside and experienced dreadful headaches; I felt that if I could just stick a needle in Mum's arm, and then one in mine the suffering would be all over for both of us. Of course I wouldn't do any such thing, but I was just so tired my thoughts were very disturbed. How lovely it would be to slip into oblivion.

I went to stay with friends in the country. I was depressed and the headaches increased; my energy levels were very low. One morning, while having a quiet time, I came across these words in the Psalms: "Sustain me according to Your promise, and I will live; do not let my hopes be dashed."[18] I thought about these words as I walked in the country lanes, I repeated them over and over like a prayer. I literally held on to them, month after month. But the hounding voice was like an attack, it increased so much; I could no longer handle the situation on my own.

I went to a counsellor to discuss the situation. She advised me that although I might reason why my husbands were taken, it didn't mean that God intended me to be brave about the tragedies. God is compassionate, not a cold impersonal being who expects us to steel our emotions and face life regardless of our feelings. She told me to give myself permission to weep for my husbands and to speak out how I missed them rather than keeping it buried. We prayed about the dark areas in my life and broke off their grip over my life in Jesus Name. Dark forces had hindered my progress. The enemy of our souls always contends with God's children when they seek to break through into new areas.

Since the darkness was addressed, there was a marked improvement. The oppression lifted, I knew a definite change within my spirit. At first, the pain of grief rising to the surface caused a heavy weight on my chest, and as I began to cry the pain seemed to tear me apart. Then I wept copiously for the two dear husbands snatched so swiftly from me.

I admitted for the first time the things I missed about them. It was the simple things that made up our lives. The romance and fun had gone out of my life. I missed the special time in the evening when the children were in bed and Eddy and I would sit by the range and talk about our day. I missed the times we walked together, sometimes talking sometimes no words were said, there was no need, just a companionable silence. I ached for his laughter, especially his ability to defuse a tension filled situation with the children. Another loss was their practical skills with D.I.Y. I wasn't very practical this way but doing things together took the hard slog out of tasks. It was such a relief to give vent to these thoughts there in that counsellor's room. She told me that whenever I felt like crying, in the days to come, to

It Happened Again

give into the feeling until my grief was assuaged.

I shared already how I was unable to bond with Esther at the time of her birth. My emotions were carefully hidden in order to face the ordeal of the birth and once I was at home I was rather relieved that she was the kind of baby that fed at regular hours and slept a lot in between; I wasn't comfortable interacting with her especially during that first year. Over the years, it was a source of grief, not a big issue, but somehow I was aware that I was slightly withdrawn from her and her needs and interests. It seemed I could never quite connect with her. I lacked spontaneity on occasions with her. Then when she moved to England to take up nursing, it was harder to connect, even with writing letters and making phone calls. When I'd visit, I would feel this frustration building up in me, that the barrier was widening and I was powerless to prevent it.

Some months after my healing, Esther came home for New Year with her husband, John. This was their first visit as a married couple. Esther and I sat together in my bedroom one afternoon, and I shared with her my inability to bond with her in her first months. With tears flowing, I spoke of the heartache I couldn't express on the day of her wedding, that her father was not present to walk her up the aisle. He would have been so proud of her. She wept too, telling me she felt cheated on that day, and in many experiences through her life. We held each other and wept our way to wholeness. We had truly bonded in our shared grief.

Each of the girls had to find healing for their own grief, even Eleanor who was born after Eddy's death. She never talked about it much until she was about fourteen years old when she was staying at her friend Kelly's house and saw Kelly sitting on her father's lap. When Eleanor returned home she told me she was upset and said to me, "Mum, I know it seems silly to be talking about my Dad this way, I never knew him. But I feel sad today because I didn't know him." Eleanor also had difficulty visiting the grave. When she got engaged to Graham, he wanted to visit his brother's grave and Eleanor wanted to know why he needed to go there. Paul wasn't there anymore. Graham helped her to see that he liked to visit the grave to remember Paul. Eleanor remembered feeling tension when we all visited Eddy's grave when she was small, because we didn't discuss feelings; she would say silly things and just wish to get out of the graveyard and go play in the park nearby. The day I brought Eleanor home from the Hospital years ago, something held me back from grieving with my children. In time, I was able to sit with them and listen to them working out their grief and weep with them. I too, found the freedom to visit the grave; where I could express emotion if I felt like it rather than feeling a stranglehold on my emotions.

There was a dual need in me. As well as dealing with grief, I was facing the empty nest. Esther and Joy had left home, and Eleanor was breaking free of the apron strings, even though she was still at home. In order to deal with this, I was very specifically led into the youngest Sunday school class, with the 2 - 5 year olds. It was not a question of what I could do for the children this time, but what they could do for me. I had taught Sunday school classes for years, with older children, and I worked hard to make those classes as interesting as possible for the children. But now, I was in need; it was enough just to be there and enjoy the little ones in their sweet innocence. In this case I was helping the teacher who had the full responsibility of the class. Making shapes with play dough and helping the children colour pictures; listening to their little stories about themselves and their families; and holding them on my lap during story time was so therapeutic. I could hardly explain this to the Sunday school staff; it was all so strange to me. I think they hoped I'd give some much-needed input into the Sunday school. But that wasn't the reason why I was there. The reason for my presence in the Sunday school room slowly unfolded from week to week, as the children, unknowingly, ministered to me.

Another layer of emotional hurt was lifted off in a Theophostic session. It was brought to light that I tried very hard in my relationship with Eddy to make sure that he wouldn't feel second best. I didn't want to compare him to my first husband. It was something I would not discuss with anyone for fear they'd get the wrong idea. The question was asked in the healing session, did I think that Eddy was second best? It wasn't so much that I thought he was second best as the fact that Eric was my first love. He had won my heart first, and I expected to spend my entire life with him. I thought it might be a betrayal of Eddy; but I came to see that it wasn't any such thing. It was only natural in remarrying that this point needed to be addressed.

The counsellor probed further to see if there was any more pain buried regarding Eric. As I went into the memories again it was observed that there was still a blockage in my emotions. I had been crying when I was first told of his death at the Hospital; and then I stopped abruptly and didn't weep again; neither at the funeral or any other occasion. With further probing I was brought back to my Granny's death and I talked through the facts that my parents didn't weep for her; they didn't discuss their feelings. There was no demonstration of grief.

It was only Isaac who had wept for her; he was the one who had discovered she had died and it had upset him greatly.

I know that they had been hurt by Granny's interference in their lives. It happened all too easily in that era when a grandmother shared the home with her family. Inevitably, there were clashes of personalities. My mother often said that she would have loved if it had been possible for Dad to get a bungalow built in one of the fields. She would have been so much happier.

I felt torn over Granny's death because I had bonded with her. She had upset me often but we had overcome this in our relationship and I genuinely missed her. I didn't know how to cope with my grief. A memory was now stirred up of the day following Granny's death; when Aunty Irene wanted to say prayers in the room where Granny was laid out. She asked me to join her; I hesitated because I was afraid of being near to the dead body. I agreed to go in; the room was terribly cold. There was no need for a fire anymore; yet the absence of one actually heightened the feeling of death. During the healing process, I had a vision of Jesus standing with us. He laid his hand of blessing upon our heads; He participated in my sorrow to such an extent that I was led into freedom in my emotions.

I was then able to return to the memory of Eric's death and experience freedom there too. I had controlled my grief so well but now I surrendered that control. The healing was remarkable because again, during the counselling session I had a picture of Jesus coming into the scene in the hospital and covering me with a warm cloak thawing out my frozen emotions.

There was one further healing which was associated with Esther's birth. As I've already written, I missed Eric sharing in the experience. Outwardly, I was smiling, but inwardly, my heart was breaking. What was significant about this healing session was the fact that I admitted I was angry that Eric had given up everything for God only for his life to be cut short. He didn't have time to welcome his baby daughter into the world. He had wanted so much to cuddle and play with his baby. I realised that deep inside of me I blamed God. This emotion had been so deep-rooted I actually had maintained for years that I didn't blame God. While I'd expressed my grief with a previous counsellor; I had not expressed my anger (I didn't even know it was there) and the lies that I had believed. I needed to get rid of the bitterness. As I asked forgiveness, I heard these words in my heart: "God doesn't want to see his children hurt; He does not cause grief willingly." The truths spoken in this session have completely cleared up this wounded area of my life. There is absolutely no shadow of grief or anger there anymore.

v). FAILURE

The fifth area was dealing with the sense of failure. Even though I knew God accepted me as I was, yet I was aware He didn't want to leave me with emotional scars. I cried buckets of tears while God's healing love began to set me free from the years of disappointment and failure connected with the music Diploma. To me it looked like an insurmountable problem. I felt I had failed miserably. It did not matter that I possessed a certificate in Advanced Senior Grade with the London College of Music. I was inconsolable. I wanted that Diploma so much.

I read somewhere that it's better to try something and fail than not to try at all. Just one small thought but it meant a great deal to me. There comes a time when one has to accept one's limitations and move on to other things. At least that's how I looked at it having read this thought, and it helped me ease up on myself to a point. This was the turning point for me in a long struggle. It would still be some years before I put it behind me. Some of my teachers had spoken, what seemed to me, careless words causing deep emotional damage. I was over sensitive having been shouted at or ignored when very small.

I often wondered why I had not faced this problem in my twenties. Thinking about it I realised I wouldn't have been able to face my problems then because I was too insecure; I would have been overwhelmed. When I grew more secure then I was able to face them. They surfaced at the right time, through divine prompting. I have heard some therapists say, leave the past alone, deal with the present. I've come to understand that the past is invariably the key to the present.

I know now I couldn't have faced it all back then. I had no sense of how I based my achieving on the approval of others. I tried to tell myself the Diploma wasn't vitally important. It didn't stop me teaching and helping my pupils to get good results in exams. I was able to work from home while my children were small. Unfortunately, I limited my intake of pupils because I felt unable to teach children beyond Grade 3. If I wished to teach music full time in a school, then an exam would be imperative. This was never my ambition.

With a change of attitude, I thought briefly of working for the Diploma in music once more, but it was dawning on me that my goals had changed in the intervening years. I didn't have the same drive to try anymore. It was suggested I try something entirely different. I thought instead, of a Word Processing course because my interest in writing was increasing, but when I applied I was told I'd have to wait four months to start. I really felt the need to fill my life with something at this point because the children were leaving home. Then it occurred to me to try Bible School. I wanted to understand the ways of God better, to understand human nature more, particularly my own nature! I wanted to make a valuable contribution to society and so I applied and was taken on immediately.

It was no easy task for a mother to return to school after years in the home but I was determined to do it. It took a lot of discipline to train my mind to hours of study and preparing essays. Just to get up in the mornings before 6a.m. to catch the College bus was a shock to the system! When I'd get home in the afternoons, I'd tumble into bed for an hour before getting a meal and settling to homework. To go to College was great healing for my self-esteem. It was a major thing for me to complete the course and obtain a diploma considering all the heartache that was connected with the music diploma, and I am so grateful to my family and friends for their support when my energy flagged; and I was assailed with doubts and felt like throwing in the towel. I loved the buzz of College life. In class, I sat between two girls, Annmarie and Sinead, the same age as my eldest daughter! I enjoyed their spontaneity and sense of fun. It was so refreshing and uplifting.

The Counselling course helped me greatly in understanding myself better. Where I battled with a sense of powerlessness in Secondary school, and in subsequent church work and did not understand my reactions; now with positive reinforcements emphasized regularly I felt empowered to serve. I was well on the road to recovery.

Following on from college, I applied to attend a writing course with the Irish Writer's Association. The only subject open just then was on how to write a novel. As a child I loved writing essays; and one was entitled "The Haunted House" which my teacher praised and offered advice on improving it.

For a long while, as an adult, I cherished writing a children's story, and once entered a short story competition. I didn't win any prizes but was encouraged by the committee to keep trying as they considered I had talent. They suggested I do a correspondence course, but as I still entertained negative thoughts about achieving, I couldn't handle it then. It was the same when I attended a local writer's club, so I withdrew. The whole thing, now, was to believe in myself.

I decided to go for the course on writing a novel until they had something more in my line. I just needed to write and string words together. I was learning to express my ideas. It was a great encouragement to be amongst other budding writers, to talk out our ambitions and frustrations and to find that the lecturer was someone who really loved her subject and was genuinely interested in our contribution in discussion and weekly homework. She knew how to draw out our own ideas and talent. Her written comments on my homework were of great value.

I read a number of interesting books on emotional well being and believed that I had dealt with emotional scars relating to failure; despite this a year or more later I had to admit my thinking was still negative regarding playing the piano. Deep down I thought I just wasn't good enough; I hadn't made the grade. I was still struggling with perfectionism; where I felt I must meet certain standards. I still looked for the approval of others; the fear of rejection dominated my actions and needed to be addressed. The ambition to achieve wasn't wrong; it was the distorted attitude that was harmful; looking for approval in the wrong place. It is better to find approval and acceptance in Christ than looking for it from other people. Then I had to learn to handle criticism; not to be so easily knocked by other people's opinions.

However I decided to try for the Diploma once again. I felt such an urge to do it but didn't see how subtle the thought was; it was actually diverting my attention from more important issues. I thought that as the children were grown now I would have more time for practise. To add to this, the Royal Academy had made changes to the Diploma regulations to allow candidates to present themselves for one section of the exam at a time i.e. to do the practical first and the theory paper later on. I decided I would work for the practical first. I learned in the local convent; my teacher was very patient and worked very hard with me keeping a clear focus on the exam requirements and also providing some books on teaching principles as there was a special section included in the exam to answer questions on the training of pupils and methods of practice etc. A month before the exam she did suggest that I should ask for advice in the Academy to see if we had covered all the work. I had already made a number of phone calls during the course and I thought this was sufficient. I felt it was too near the exam to make any changes. I never worked so hard for an exam before; even though I gave it my best shot my best was not good enough. I fell far short of the pass mark. I took it badly; I thought the examiner had marked unfairly; at the same time I regretted not taking the teacher's advice.

In November of that year, we went to the States for a Conference; while I was there I had a dream that I was back in school and I had to recite a poem. I went along with the arrangement until the last moment but I hadn't learned it. I wondered would I make a fool of myself standing up in front of everyone and having nothing to say. I didn't even know what poem it was. I backed out at the last moment. I told the teacher that I wasn't reciting the poem. I told her I didn't have to do it. I felt quite strong about it. I went to Dublin instead (still in the dream) I heard there was a concert some place and came across the venue and I was sorry I'd missed most of it, they were having such a good time.

My first reaction to the dream, on waking, was that it referred to my music; because the pressure I felt to recite and perform was like a friend's experience where he had recurring dreams of facing an exam and not being ready. What a relief it would be to give the idea of an exam up. I decided I'd drop it. In January, with the new school term, I doubted the interpretation of the dream; I wondered how I could have interpreted "poem" as an exam. Along with the doubts came the urge to try again. I was growing weary of the struggle but I didn't know how to lay it down. My children thought that I was obsessed with it; and that I should simply enjoy the music. I had a slight sense of unease some of the time but somehow I lacked the insight and confidence to stop. Some friends and family advised me to keep pressing on. There was a confusion of voices and it was very difficult to hear the right one.

I returned to studying this time with a teacher under the London College of Music. The teacher read the exam results, and then sized up my ability for a few weeks. She told me she agreed with the examiner's mark in the Academy. Then she showed me how to improve my scale playing and was quite severe on getting me to improve my technique. I took with all the stringent measures hoping that I could improve but it was tough. I also studied one of Bach's Preludes and Fugues in preparation for the exam. She provided me with a list of book titles on teaching principles that enlarged my thinking further on teaching piano.

One day she said that I shouldn't think of doing an exam but rather enjoy the music. It would be far better to think of how best to teach music, and give my pupils a good foundation. Study to be a good teacher and don't focus on an exam, it's not the be-all and end-all of everything. I welcomed this discussion and opened up about an area that perplexed me. I remarked, "The world makes such a big thing of achieving in exams and competing." She replied, "Only if you let it." I told her I'd grown very nervous with having failed so often. She asked me why I wanted to put myself through that again. She felt she'd be failing in her duty if she didn't correct my technique and she hoped that the rigorous training hadn't put me off. She also mentioned that if a pupil of hers barely passed Grade 8 she would not allow them to prepare for a Diploma examination. This reminded me that, years ago, I had barely passed my Grade 8 and yet the teacher prepared me for Diploma. I had tried so hard to make up for the loss of marks by repeating the exam for Diploma standard so often but to no avail. This was my moment of truth.

I went home and thought over what she said; and then I remembered the dream I'd had in November. Upon reflection, I thought that where I had dreamt of going back to school represented a current learning experience that was my music. While I pondered on the dream, a friend had a dream that seemed to confirm my dream. In the dream he was at a cemetery. There were two horses with two carts but he didn't see the coffin. They were waiting for the "coffin – person" to come. He saw that someone had pulled back a cloth off one of the carts and the coffin was there. There were old books in the other cart. My friend wandered around the place looking for the person, then he heard the right music being played and knew it was time to start the funeral service; the person must have arrived. (He had heard music earlier, but it wasn't the right music). I trusted this friend and the insight he received concerning me.

As soon as I heard music mentioned in the dream that got my attention. The books were big enough to be music scores. I came to see that this dream was a message to me from God to bury my ambition regarding a diploma and to bury my thick music books. It didn't mean that I was going to give up music completely, or stop teaching, but simply for my own personal benefit to play the music that I enjoy (light classical; Irish songs and Ballads; some pop and hymns.) Good-bye heavy classical; give me fun songs and spiritual songs any day and I am happy.

I returned the next week and told the teacher that I wanted to drop the idea of doing an exam and instead I wanted to increase my ability in preparing children for grade work. I have taught successfully from beginners to Grade 3 with good exam results. If I had sat for the ALCM (TD) I would have had to make a presentation of showing how I would teach children from beginners to Grade Five. Now I asked the teacher to work with me on Grade Four and Grade Five. Sometime later, I wrote out my presentation as if preparing for an exam so that I would have this information at my fingertips and could "present" it to my pupils as the occasion arose in their classes. At the end of term I knew I had attended my last piano lesson. The message in the dreams had satisfied me and put an end to my obsession.

I know that while I spent many hours practising each day I did find it extremely difficult to be focused. A pianist needs to be single minded. I was working on two movements in Mozart's Sonata in G, K283, there were a number of ornaments included in the Andante section which are small notes that have to be played into the given time signature. The result should be fluent trills. I spent much time on this; repeating the sequence over and over again. And still I couldn't perfect it. It required more time and expertise than I could muster. I am learning to accept that I am a dreamer; I like to think deeply about life issues and write down my thoughts. I found that the two interests clashed.

It has been a long struggle to discover where my gifts and talents lie but I think it is time for closure in this area of exams. It is very hard to give up a cherished ambition. I trust that I have laid it down for the last time. Always before, when I'd fail an exam I'd get so disheartened that I'd dismiss everything about music. But then I was denying the creative longing and talent within me. This time, I have increased my teaching experience up to Grade Five. I can also provide alternative lessons for pupils interested in learning electronic keyboard.

I look at the positives in my life; I have passed music theory for Diploma standard and can do much with this. I was told about a certain college student who failed one subject in his degree course. Although he was naturally very disappointed he couldn't go on to teach as planned; he didn't allow this to stop him getting a good job in a managerial position. It is possible to make use of our learning when channelled in a slightly different route to what we first planned. For some who fail, it's good that they be encouraged to bring out the talent that lies within them. For others, like me, who have tried many times and failed, it is time to find other avenues for success.

I think that there is much to look forward to; as my own dream indicated. A "concert" was in progress and the people present were having such a good time. There was no orchestra or singing group there; but the message was definitely conveyed to me that there was a concert going on and I was sorry that I had missed most of it. I felt it had some connection with the freedom of the Spirit of God. The concert was held in "Dublin" and that was another puzzle. Yet I couldn't see what these things meant for some time.

I had to search out the hidden meaning. I've noticed that people in Scripture often had to search diligently for the meaning to their dreams. The pictures in dreams are mostly symbolic; only very occasionally are they literal. I learned that there are standard meanings to symbols given in dreams, but there are also some symbols given that are unique to the individual. I came to see that to be in "concert" means people moving in harmony together and listening to the conductor or organiser who, in this case, is the Holy Spirit. "Dublin" as a symbol represented something that was unique to me in that when I was a teenager I chose to live in Dublin where I could pursue my interest in the Holy Spirit. When I finally saw the meaning, that I had not listened to the Spirit concerning my music, I was sorry I had taken so long to realise it (just like in the dream). There was something good going on in the dream that I wanted to be a part of and I am confident that I will learn to move under the direction of the Holy Spirit in this area and so fulfil my destiny.

And so finally, I understand that failure, in the light of God's reckoning, is not failure at all but a stepping stone to freedom and success.

VI). LIVING BY THE RULES

The final area to deal with was legalism. It tripped me up regularly. It affected me in so many ways. It put me on so many guilt trips. Legalism took the form of being caught up in rules and regulations from an early age with its focus on good works. You must say your prayers every night. You must go to church every Sunday. You must put money in the offering and support missionaries. You must keep the Sabbath holy. All good advice, but detrimental when continually drummed into you in an autocratic manner. I've seen this sort of thing turn people away from God.

The outward rules were adhered to more for fear of what other people would think rather than God. It was important how one dressed, how tidy your home was kept, what school you attended and how you achieved at that school. You were put on a guilt trip regularly, if you didn't carry out the rules. Your friends were scrutinized and weighed up and often found wanting. It continued relentlessly into choosing a career. The ongoing standards, the ongoing worry, "what will people think." My Granny was like Hyacinth in the T.V. serial, "Keeping Up Appearances," she would exasperate us in her efforts to keep a high profile in the community. It was a fear of man, basing your behaviour on other people's opinions. It controlled our lives. It was subtly woven into our thinking. I felt I was pulled in all directions, when I focused on people seeking their approval. Granny had pushed the proper way to do things down our necks. It made me fussy, over conscientious, and I tended to complicate everything.

I adopted some more legalistic attitudes at boarding school, I gathered that the appropriate behaviour for a Christian woman was that she shouldn't wear make-up, or wear trousers. She should wear a hat in church. She should not go to dances or take a drink. I also got the impression that it wasn't good to watch television.

Later, I came to see that these rules were man made and not necessarily God intended. I know that many parents are concerned for their children regarding dancing and drinking because of the destructive influences. I don't intend to get into a big discussion here, but I would just say that these things are not harmful in themselves if they are enjoyed in moderation and if young people are encouraged to make friends with those who will have a positive influence on their lives. The rule about no drinking suited me because I hated alcohol for what it did to my father. Eric and Eddy had no hang-ups about drink; they enjoyed a glass of wine on special occasions. I joined in but was torn inside. Living alone, I was a total abstainer for years, until I was reminded that Jesus attended a wedding once and turned water into wine. If I was a guest at that wedding, and everyone was exclaiming about the miracle I'd want to taste that marvellous wine too. Having said all that, if a recovered alcoholic were a guest in my house, I would be sensitive to their needs.

These rules are legalistic and actually cause many young people to enter a different kind of bondage from that which Christ had freed them from in the first place. Surely it is more helpful to follow sound advice, that we don't walk in the counsel of the ungodly; [19] rather than separating ourselves from some pleasures that God actually gave us to enjoy. Despite these difficulties, the essential part of the change in my life was genuine and has remained through thick and thin. The legalistic elements almost suffocated the life of Christ within me, until I came to a better understanding of the issues.

By degrees I eased up on these restrictions. It was a great day when I got rid of the hats. I felt like jumping on them and tearing them to shreds. Mine were frightful things, because I used to buy them simply because I had to wear one, not for how they looked. I'd go into a shop, grab one off a stand, pay for it scrunch it up in a bag and take it home. I'd never think about

It Happened Again

the colour or shape. Then I'd straighten it out on Sunday, place it on my head and go to church. When it slowly dawned on me that they didn't match my outfits, I wondered how I ever dared walk down the street in such ludicrous things. To this day I absolutely hate hats.

Another restricted area was television. I was always in a dilemma over television. At first, when I went home on school holidays I wouldn't watch it at all. My family thought I was peculiar. Eric cut across that erratic behaviour by settling down to a good film whenever he visited the farm. He wasn't bound by rules. But for some years, I battled on, sometimes I favoured having a T.V. as a single parent, other times, in exasperation, I'd sell it.

Activities on Sunday were another legal bind. When my own children were growing up, they often chaffed against the restrictions I put upon them. One rule was you're not allowed do homework on Sunday. Sometimes it was forgotten on Saturday and that irritated me because they'd want to do it Sunday. On other occasions there were genuine reasons, they just couldn't finish an essay on Saturday, or they needed to read some History or work on some project such as doing a plan of a local shopping mall. I would argue the point about observing the rule about Sunday. The girls thought it was a silly rule, and said Sundays were boring. How much easier it would have been to give in, the children would have been better occupied. The laugh was on me when I started going to Bible College and ended up doing my homework on Sundays!

For a long time there was tension regarding these areas. It wasn't until a fresh breeze of the Spirit of God came to us in Dublin '94, from the Airport Vineyard church in Toronto that I, personally, found the wrappings of legalism being lifted off me.

There were great questions raised, naturally, about the things that were happening there. I, too, questioned and was very wary and puzzled by the action of some people claiming to have been blessed by God. The behaviour of some of them left a lot to be desired. It was over the top. For instance, God was birthing new things in people, intercessory prayer and new ministries and in the large groups I attended in St. Marks and Werburgh St. people were groaning loudly with this birthing taking place deep inside them. Unfortunately, some people seemed to be faking it, copying the genuine and it grated on folk turning some right off it.

It was also a time of laughter and tears, and you soon learned to distinguish between the copy and the genuine thing. The genuine laughter was infectious, and so deeply satisfying, the copy rang hollow; the same also with the tears. But was I going to ignore it just because some were over the top? After I carefully weighed up my questions and read some historical accounts of strange behaviour in revivals and modern day testimonies, and asked for guidance to know what was real and what was sham, I relaxed then and began to enjoy the blessing.

I was reminded of a dream I had the summer of '94 when news was just filtering through of great things happening in Toronto. I had gone away alone in June for a weekend in Wicklow to a lovely B/B situated on a hill overlooking Brittas Bay. I was feeling stressed out at the end of the school year with carrying responsibility for the girls, and my involvement in church activities. I longed for peace and quiet, to restore my equilibrium. It turned out I was the only guest for the whole weekend, so my desire for peace was very much satisfied. I felt very much the need to lighten up and enjoy a hearty laugh. I told the Lord I could do with a large helping of joy before I returned home.

Early the following morning I had a comical dream about three men in a forest. One man wanted to be playful, and to help his mates to lighten up. He reached down to pick up some soil and started spreading it on his face. He wanted to involve his friends. He was daring them to let go and have fun. His two friends surrendered to a fun game of wrestling and then they rubbed his belly. Suddenly, I woke up laughing, amused at the dream and feeling a bit foolish because I felt my belly had been rubbed too. I stifled the laughter as I remembered where I was, always too conscious of others and easily inhibited. Immediately, I regretted it, because it was such a good feeling. And I thought of my request for joy the day before. Why did I have to spoil it?

The interpretation came to me much later. I think the Holy Spirit was answering my prayer, as he was beginning to do for many Christians around that time, he wanted to loosen me up, "rub" my "belly", tickle me, that's what he wanted to do in effect, and bring forth laughter. After all, didn't Jesus promise, "Out of your belly shall flow rivers of living water."[20] The word "belly" might offend some, it's just the literal translation used by the King James Version to indicate the centre of our spirit. When Jesus uttered those words he was talking about the Holy Spirit flooding people with joy and equipping them with power to witness, to serve, to live life to the full.

For months, I watched mostly from the sidelines as the blessing from Toronto spread through some of our churches in Dublin. I observed others entering into freedom but I would tighten up as I witnessed others making, what I considered, an exhibition of themselves. You wouldn't catch me behaving like that, I thought. Secretly, I longed to be just as free as they were, enjoying themselves. God knew all about my inhibitions, and made it easy for me. He used someone else who was having a good time, in the seat in front of me. The man's laughter was so infectious, he just gave himself up to joyful abandonment. I was drawn irresistibly into the laughter. It was not just a cause and effect sort of thing, I was aware of God in it, I had no doubt, and there was a power behind it and a refreshing anointing. I had a hard time trying to sit straight in my chair. After awhile I didn't mind that I felt a little drunk.

I wrestled with my church background; surely it's undignified to go to such extremes? However I came to see that in the same way that I enjoy fellowship with my family; our get-togethers; picnics and outings; where there is lots of laughter, noise and informality, so I realised that the family reflects the same relationship that God desires to have with us. God has a sense of humour and it is quite acceptable to express laughter in His Presence even in church. God was working deep down at the core of my being helping me to lighten up, renewing me, healing me after many years of spiritual drought. I was hot, dusty, and very, very thirsty. Now that thirst was being quenched. He was reminding me that church doesn't have to be stiff and starchy. I think a lot of people had had religion up to their ears and now they were finding church could be fun!

One thing that was proclaimed in some of these meetings was "Let mercy triumph over judgement." The voice of mercy was heard, not the critical, judging spirit that has dominated some of our Christian churches. The voice of mercy speaks in loving and gracious tones. How much greater to show love instead of always feeling you have to correct and find fault? There is a place for correction, I know, but mostly God's way is

"A gentle answer turns away wrath."[21] It was said prophetically, of our Lord "And Your lips have been anointed with grace."[22] He is our example and He brought the refreshing of His Holy Spirit into some churches during this period.

Some people remained caught up with appearances rather than welcoming the joy of the free gospel of Christ. Others again were caught up in activity rather than cultivating loving, heart-felt relationships. There was one thing that didn't add up for me, how Christians would say it's great to serve the Lord yet so many, including myself, were struggling to serve the Lord. I remember, as a child, hearing part of a prayer said in the Church of Ireland, "...whose service is perfect freedom." Freedom? What freedom? It hadn't quite turned out the way I expected. And from the accounts of others I knew many experienced depression and tears, breakdown of health, burnout. For me, it was an ongoing battle and discussions about appropriate behaviour for Christians especially my own daughters. As I hadn't gone dancing as a teenager, apart from a couple of church socials, I wondered how I should handle the situation now? Would I allow them to attend the school disco, for instance? I tried to talk them out of it, but with Joy and Eleanor they were very keen to go, and I gave in because I knew that there were teachers supervising. When they grew older and left school, they wanted to go dancing occasionally and have a drink with their boyfriends. Now was the time that I had to let go and allow them to make up their own minds.

As I said, I was a "Rules" oriented person. No matter how hard I tried, I kept falling into the trap of following rules, arguing over this and that and getting my brain in a knot. I just went too hard at everything. I wore myself out. With the "Toronto" blessing I couldn't keep legalistic ways anymore. I noticed this phenomenon with my approach to exams, and I couldn't diet in the same way anymore. The move of God's Spirit brought relaxation in me, He began to sweep away all the stuffy standards and observances. For a time it upset my framework for life, that I had so carefully constructed. I noticed it particularly in Bible College.

During the first year I followed the curriculum in a tightly controlled manner. Secretly, I wished I had said I'd only do one year, the exams were such a strain. Anyway, I started into the second year and try as I might I just couldn't approach the course in the same way. Two months into the term I thought I was falling apart. For the first time in my life I approached the staff, something I'd run miles from during my schooldays. And I wept in front of them, another thing I could control before but not now. I didn't communicate very well at first, and I'm sure they were baffled at this turn of events. I didn't seem to have any trouble the first year so what was happening now. They made helpful suggestions once they realised I was struggling and very slowly, I adapted to a less pressured form of study and approach to exams.

In reality, this falling apart was a time of being broken before the Lord, but before I grasped how much God was in it, I thought I was going off the deep end. I felt I was losing my grip on God, if I can put it that way, my understanding of him, my experiences with him over the years. Didn't it account for anything now? Why did I feel so disturbed?

I also felt I was losing my confidence when asked to do the simplest of things or make a decision. While I had a tight control on things, I often seemed unapproachable to people. During this time when I was "falling apart" and started opening up to some of the women in Beulah, the Christian Single Parent group, one woman regarded me, speechless, and then she said, "I can't believe this. You always gave the impression of having it altogether." While I seemed to have it together, I couldn't communicate effectively with people who expressed their real needs. It wasn't until I broke down and finally attempted to communicate that I bonded with the group.

This took place during a weekend away together in Newcastle. The main thing I remember of that weekend is the speaker saying prophetically to us all that there would no longer be a blockage in our lives touching on friendships and freedom of expression. During the invigorating experience in the ministry time, afterwards, I was given a personal word: There is a calling on your life to speak. You've thought that it was for others, but it is for you too, you are free.

Some thought I'd gone very religious when I was converted as a teenager. This time of coming into contact with God initially set me free; but I was hindered by the legalistic views of a group of people. Now as an adult caught up in this refreshing move of God I was coming into a freedom to be myself. I can now understand when Jesus brought Lazarus forth from the dead that he turned to the people around him, and said, "Loose Him"[23]. Surely this is the work of the church. Jesus gives new life but equips the church to set people free.

During this period of brokenness, my pastor asked me to take part in an Outreach weekend. He thought I'd be a useful member on the team. I had my doubts because I felt so broken. How could I be of any use? Yet with some basic training in College and going out as part of a team I was better prepared. There was a series of meetings over the weekend including a street meeting. I was so much more comfortable this time compared to the Outreach in Wales. I simply did what I was comfortable with; I played the keyboard with the worship team or sometimes played alone as people went up for prayer; there was just such a sense of the Presence of God. Other times I sat and listened to people when they wanted to talk.

After the evening meeting; as people came up for prayer, members of the team went to pray with them. I knew without a doubt on one occasion that there was one person I should stand beside and pray for her. There was a witness deep in my spirit, and I bonded with this woman who was crushed by some dominant folk in her church. As she wept under the weight of this grief, the Holy Spirit began to heal and lift her burden. I simply knelt beside her and wept along with her. In our shared brokenness, Jesus drew very near to both of us. This was a breakthrough for me and I was able to go on two further outreach trips.

There were some wonderful songs written during this time of God's outpouring, expressing something of the softening and relaxing that God was showing His people. Sometimes I couldn't even sing along with everyone because the tears were flowing down my face with the relief that was filling my whole being. All the stiff and starchy effects of legalism were being washed out of my system. Then another night during the singing I'd have the strangest feelings of wanting to do crazy things, long forgotten in childhood. To do nonsensical things like a game of Leapfrog or Turn the Wildcat, or roll head over heels downhill in the long grass, like we did in the fields long ago; to abandon my inhibitions and let go. Laughter began to well up. For no specific reason, it just felt so good as I thought on these things. I felt the freedom and anticipation of a child once again. My soul was liberated from years of repression.

For each of these six areas where there were sad experiences resulting in distorted thinking, Jesus replaced them with truth and allowed me to experience His infinite love and compassion for He entered completely into each situation and dispelled the darkness and thoroughly healed the emotional pain. He has given me a new confidence based on the sure knowledge that Jesus is the Source of my strength. The past does not haunt me anymore; I can walk away from it free in the knowledge and reality of Christ's forgiveness and power.

TWELVE

A dream comes true

ON MY RETURN from the Beulah weekend (Single Parents) in Nov '97, I had the distinct impression that my partner would turn up in the near future. How or when I had no idea, I just knew a change was imminent.

I thought the main work in my healing was at an end, but I think that once I had opened myself up to the Healer the restoration continued indefinitely. I busied myself with such activities as helping a friend run a Good News Club for the children in our neighbourhood; doing reception work in our church office and enjoying the Writing course.

Many times over the years, while I waited for the promise to be fulfilled, I was tempted to doubt. Sometimes, I asked myself, "Are you sure this is not just wishful thinking?" While staying in the B/B in Brittas Bay the same weekend I asked for the gift of joy, I also prayed about the delay. I had to be sure that I had received a real promise from God and that I was not indulging in daydreams.

As I prayed, God reminded me of the promise given. I had doubted because of the long delay. In the beginning, when the promise was fresh I was curious, looking around every corner for this promised husband. Then when time passed and he never showed up, I dragged my feet. Now, I asked God to help me maintain a balance. Still, the years passed, and I seriously considered joining a Christian dating agency, but God whispered to hold on and allow Him to bring it about. I would have been happy just to start a correspondence with a male friend, not necessarily dating.

I hoped my relationship with God wouldn't change, if I got married. It was very important to me that God remain first in my life. I esteemed Him above all others. He was my best friend. Anyone who married me would have to understand this. It wasn't so clear to me in my previous marriages, but now it was essential to any relationship I would form.

I fully expected a stranger to appear. As there was a shortage of eligible men for my age group within the circles I moved, I reckoned God could give me another Englishman or hunt further afield for a husband! I used to think it was possible he was busy tying up his affairs, packing, getting ready to leave his country and move to Ireland. Can you imagine my surprise when the prospective husband turned out to be a long-standing friend of the family now living in the West of Ireland!

On November 8th 1997, I had a strong feeling that something was about to happen that would affect my future. I forgot all about this impression when a week later I heard the sad news that Joy Gray had died after a long struggle with cancer. All my sympathy was stirred when I saw John stand at the front of the church the day of the funeral. John had given up his teaching career and pastoral work to spend more time with his wife. He had left friends and church following a leading from God to move to Galway, believing he would be involved in some work there. And what had happened? Just eleven months after moving, Joy was dead.

John was stunned, for he had believed Joy was improving;

her medication had been reduced by half only weeks before her death. His dream was shattered. What could God be thinking of? It seemed too much to think of ministry without the help of his wife. During the funeral service, a prophetic word was spoken, to this effect: "You may think it is the end, but it is only the beginning. I will use what has happened and will pour the oil of healing upon the family and make them a blessing."

John and Joy had stood with me in my hour of need. Now, John needed support. I listened to John as he tried to describe the awful gap he experienced after sharing his life with Joy for 34 years. Both John and I realised that God was bringing two lonely people together. The ache in my heart corresponded to the ache in John's heart. I was facing the empty nest, my three girls had grown independent, and I, too, was facing an awful gap. Eddy's Mum said to me, "Now that your girls are independent, is there a Sugar-Daddy who would take you under his wing and spoil you!" I think God was working on it. The Perfect Matchmaker guided us! I would like to share some of the wonderful assurances we received in taking steps towards marriage, for it was very important to us that we were making the right decision before God.

In 1991, when God first led me to pray specifically for a husband, I asked him to show me who he was, to bring about a meeting between us. And when the wheels would be set in motion, getting acquainted, love blossoming, etc, then to give us an inner sense of God's direction. I also asked that God would give me confirmation from two independent sources that we were doing the right thing. This was a third marriage for me and I didn't want to make a mistake.

In the circumstances, it wasn't possible for God to show me who the man was way back in '91. God knew there would be a delay. I made that request thinking the man would be a perfect stranger, and that if God wasn't willing to reveal his identity then, perhaps, he'd give me some indication or sign so that when the man appeared I would know he was God's intended. I had a dream in November '94, containing a message, laid out like an application form:

Name: Helen (no surname)

Age: not clear

Address: 31 Ballygall Crescent, Finglas East, Dublin 11.

Occupation: Of her own volition

Message: A brother - He is on his way - He is just around the corner

I thought it very peculiar. But then dreams are often peculiar. I had to look up the dictionary to see what 'volition' meant, and discovered it meant "act or faculty of willing." I wasn't teaching at the time, mainly engaged in church work. It made sense to say "of her own volition" because it was activities I willingly got involved in.

As for the message itself, I speculated on it a lot. We use the term "just around the corner" when talking of someone who lives close by yet I didn't know any widower or eligible single man living close by. We also use this expression "just around the corner" in terms of time, meaning an event will take place quite soon. The word 'brother' I understood to mean a Christian person who would be a companion, helpmate and support. I took it to mean I would meet a husband quite soon. Little did I know that it did actually mean distance as well as time, that for many years John lived just five minutes car drive from my house.

I waited four more years, and finally God set events in motion. I was reluctant to strike up a relationship with John at first. During the Christmas period, my daughter Joy remem-

A dream comes true

bered John was now facing his first Christmas without his wife. She wanted to make contact with him to let him know we were thinking of him; she suggested I phone and we both chat with him. From Joy's point of view there was always that bond with "uncle John" as the children had called him. I really had a hard time with this suggestion because I was so aware that our positions had changed. John was now a widower and I was a widow and I didn't want anyone to think I was looking for a relationship. It was the furthest thing from my mind to see a future with him; I believed God had other plans, I didn't see His leading at this time. Reluctantly, I phoned for Joy's sake.

At the end of January '98 John invited me and Joy to the "month's mind" that he held in Dublin in memory of his wife; and after the meeting he and Joy were chatting and Joy innocently said she'd love to go visit him in Galway. Then John drew me into the conversation by suggesting we should all visit. To Joy it was keeping up the link of friendship. I felt caught and for the sake of that friendship I went along with the arrangement. In a way, Joy played cupid in this romance!

It was quite a poignant weekend staying with John and Pauline who had come down from Belfast for the few days. Everywhere in the house I could see evidence of Joy's life; most of all her lace work which she had enjoyed so much. It just seemed so unfair that she had developed cancer; if only God had healed her so that she and John could fulfil their destiny together! It was during this visit that John took tentative steps towards a relationship with me. I refused to see it, I tried to tell myself that John was talking about some other widow; and could hardly wait to get on the bus Sunday afternoon. Two things stood out that day; as we waited for the bus to move I watched John as he walked away across Eyre Sq. and I felt an awful pang in the pit of my stomach as I thought of him returning to an empty house and I wondered how he would bear it. Then I put it all out of my mind until the bus drew near to Dublin; and a small voice whispered in my spirit: "It's you John was talking about". As the days unfolded I gradually became convinced that this was God's plan.

John and I were drawn together by divine prompting at first, and then we noticed that friendship was rapidly turning into love. It took us by surprise and especially the growing urgency to get married soon. Therefore it meant a lot that God answered my prayer made years before, to give me confirmation from two independent sources. What I mean by this, is that God would reveal to two individuals whom I could trust, some thought of reference to our present circumstances without them knowing that we were considering getting married. Then I would have no doubt that God was directing us.

I received the first confirmation at our local house group in the home of Joe and Jackie Fitzgerald, Finglas (Mar'98). Peter Finch, a pastor from Calvary Church, was visiting and gave me a personal prophetic word: "Don't be afraid to ask and believe for the desires of your heart. He will give you the desires of your heart. For he has not given you the spirit of fear, but of love, power and a sound mind." I just knew that this was referring to my relationship with John. It came with a force and anointing that left me in no doubt. Comparing notes with John later, I found that he had received almost the identical words from Peter the night before at a meeting he had attended in town. We needed to be told not to fear, for if we married just months after Joy's death, we would be going against the tide of opinion. Both family and friends would find it difficult to understand.

A dream comes true

How can a person marry someone else so soon after losing a partner? Only those who have lost can answer that question. To those looking on it looks like a betrayal or lack of respect. Yet the partner left behind didn't choose to be left alone. Death cut across their plans. They wanted to remain married and enjoy old age together. Instead they found themselves alone. We are all social creatures with a need to be loved, a need for companionship. Some people choose to "be faithful to the memory of their first spouse" as they put it and don't marry again. I commend them for their decision.

But for those who enter a second marriage it doesn't mean they are unfaithful to their first spouse. John and I hold our previous marriages as treasured memories and they have a special place in our hearts. We chose to marry for love and companionship and much more, it was a question of the leading and timing of God. I had a need to be married when the children were small, but it was not appropriate then to marry someone, more to the point, it was not God's time.

It is customary to wait an appropriate time before remarriage out of respect for the former partner. However, John received his own assurances that he was taking the right step. John's friend Bill Turner, whose prophetic ministry John had come to trust over the years had accurately guided John's care and ministry to Joy in her latter months. Now at Joy's death the Lord showed John that the way ahead for him would be "golden" though for a time it would be "grey." This puzzled, even angered John. "How could the way ahead be "golden"? I've just lost my life's partner." However because John trusted Bill's word and another friend and minister, Keith Gerner, confirmed it, John allowed the word to settle in his spirit. Knowing that God had brought him to Galway after 30 years of waiting and that a new ministry awaited him, the thought began to form in his mind, "Is God saying I should get remarried. I can't see myself in the ministry again without a partner?" And so he made contact with me.

I wanted to be really sure we were doing the right thing and in May of that year I received a strong conviction that Joy was now safe with God; there was no need to fret on her account. God was now concerned for John's well being and I was not to be afraid to take this step in marriage as soon as possible.

It is usually advised that a bereaved person, for their own sake, wait a period of at least two years before they get married again. People said John might be in need of counselling to get back on his feet. We were running any number of risks. Yet John did not bottle up his grief, but wept freely when he felt like it and so the process of grieving was not delayed. As I had already lost two husbands some people were concerned for John that he might be the third, however, John felt this marriage was of God and so what people said didn't concern him.

He was well able to handle various comments; for example, a nurse in the Regional Hospital in Galway who remarked: "I hate men like you who look around for another wife and marry so quickly". John told her he didn't go dating; he knew me for many years and his first thought concerning me was for friendship and companionship. The nurse accepted this better. It was pointed out to me that in many cases a widower was more likely to marry quickly than a widow; and then I read a magazine article supporting this view.

For all this, it was becoming clear that God had chosen to bring us together now. It was His purpose to bring two people together, who had both suffered loss, and establish us as a couple in preparation for the ministry He had appointed in the very near future. I was not a substitute wife; the marriage was very much planned by God.

The second confirmation came the night I shared about my inner healing at St. Mark's (April '98). It was such a pleasure to share of the tremendous healing taking place in my life. As I spoke, the power and anointing of God rested upon me. Afterwards, a number of people came to speak to me, rejoicing with me that I had succeeded in speaking, for I had felt under great strain for days beforehand. It's often that way when you're about to share something of significance in your life, the enemy of our soul makes it extremely difficult.

Amongst those who spoke with me was Marie Gough. I knew Marie well having worked together with her on a worship team for many months. She told me my testimony was powerful and she spoke about a new marriage, and with this marriage the healing would be complete. Marie frequently prophesied in our meetings; and as she spoke now to me it sounded just like a prophecy and witnessed with my spirit. There was a note of excitement in her voice. She assured me she was praying for a godly man for me. All this without a word from me of what was happening between John and I; this was confirmation indeed. I explained the whole thing to her at a later date, after I had shared the two words of confirmation with John.

In the months leading up to John and I forming a relationship, my prayer times were punctuated with tears for the unknown partner. I wondered, sometimes, what difficulties he was facing and why I felt such heartache. Now I knew the reason for these intercessions and why they were so emotional, for I was weeping for John's bereavement. Since I was so recently healed from repressed grief, it was like when John came on the scene, that I felt I had been recently bereaved too, the same as him. The memories were fresh with me and I was filled with compassion and sympathy for him. It bonded us together as nothing else could.

It's interesting to note that John's qualities and characteristics fit my list of requirements in every respect. He is an attractive man with a teasing sense of humour. He has an appreciation of music, and plays the recorder occasionally. He enjoys worshipping God. He understands about cherishing his wife and nurturing an intimate relationship. He is excellent with D.I.Y. and gardening. He is some years older than myself, has three children, two daughter-in-laws, one son-in-law and two grandchildren. As for the request about someone to take Eleanor on an outing to fly a kite, now that she's married we'll leave that to her husband!

Now God was bringing John and I together to serve Him in Galway. Six weeks before our wedding we met with my pastor and his wife, Gary and Wilma Davidson. We discussed scriptures for the wedding service and prayed together. In an encouraging prophecy Gary gave, the Holy Spirit assured us of the blessing of God upon our lives, and that out of the love and passion we have for each other our ministry would grow and bless others. This benediction was like the icing on the cake.

I think of my friends in Beulah. They gave me a wonderful Hen Party a few weeks before the wedding. I received many cards and presents. I know that it wasn't easy for some to attend such an occasion. They put on a brave smile that night. It was hard for them to hear that one of the group was getting remarried. While they were happy for me, naturally, they'd love it if they could marry again. Engagements and weddings are difficult occasions for a single person to bear when all the good things seem to be happening to someone else.

One woman said to me later, "It's O.K. for you. You're enjoying the benefits of married life." As if moving from the ranks of single parent to the ranks of the married meant that I was worlds apart from them. Yes, in one sense that's true but I am a married person with a difference. I want to say to my friends that I will never forget that I was a single parent. To do so would be ignoring almost 20 years of my life. It has moulded and shaped me into the person I am today. I walked where they walked. "I've done that, I've worn the T-shirt!" I can empathise with the single parent; I know how she thinks and feels.

Another thing I cannot forget is that I've lived in a Corporation flat for many years and the restrictions I experienced there. Just because I'm living in a big house now doesn't mean that I've made it to some level that sets me above the rest. If I was tempted to think this was the case, I only have to remind myself that all this has come at a great cost; the death of two husbands, and for John the death of his wife. We have joined our resources together to purchase a property that we see will enable us to carry out our vision for ministry, to use it as a centre to bring restoration to broken lives. We felt from the start we had to share what God was giving us because it was so obvious that it's too big for just the two of us.

I remember thinking that if I married again; it would not be to live a life wrapped up in my new partner, no matter how tempting that might be after being alone so long. No, I thought if I had the chance it would be to live a useful life of service to reach out to others who hurt like I hurt, and pray their lives would be restored to complete wholeness.

I write to women who have suffered the loss of a partner. I know that because I was widowed I cannot identify in one area with many single parents. Death is final. For me there was a cut off point but for single parents who have been separated or divorced, this is not so. The husband is alive and this in itself could have profound emotional consequences especially where there are children involved. Yet there are many similarities whether widowed or divorced and that is why I share my story with you, to let you know, this need not be the end. Perhaps you have lost your home and everything dear to you, maybe you feel you're losing control of your life and are in deep turmoil. You can experience the glory and power of God in a way that will transform your life and give you the hope and the will to succeed; to live your life again filled with direction and purpose. The power of God's love can triumph over the greatest heartache, be it death or divorce.

It takes the fulfilment of just one dream to get us on our feet and moving forward. Two dreams have come true for me; to live in the country and to get married again, a third one is in process; the writing of this book. My faith has grown. As surely as these two events have taken place so I believe all the rest of God's promises concerning me will follow in His time.

Notes

CHAPTER 1
1. John 14:12
2. Isaiah 41:10 (KJV)
3. Luke 11:31 (KJV)

CHAPTER 2
1. 2 Kings 3:16 –20
2. Philippians 1:21 (KJV)
3. Isaiah 55:8 (KJV)
4. John 13:7 (KJV)
5. Psalms 16:11
6. Psalms 124: 7
7. Esther 4:14b; 7:3,4
8. John 12:24
9. Job 1:9
10. Psalms 139:16

CHAPTER 3
1. John 11:25
2. John 13:7
3. Deuteronomy 8:2
4. 1Peter 1:7

CHAPTER 4
1. Psalm 68:5; 146:9; 10:17

It Happened Again

2. 1Peter 5:8
3. Ephesians 6: 12-14

CHAPTER 5
1. John 14:2
2. Revelation 4: 1-6; 5:11-14
3. 1 Thessalonians 4:13-18
4. Psalm 16:11
5. Luke 23:43
6. Leviticus 19: 31
7. Isaiah 8:19

CHAPTER 6
1. Hebrews 4:12
2. John 4: 13,14
3. Matthew 8:20
4. Hebrews 4: 15
5. Luke 15: 11-32

CHAPTER 7
1. Psalm 91: 11
2. Psalm 34:7
3. Revelation 5: 11; Hebrews 1:14
4. Colossians 1: 6; 2: 18
5. Isaiah 14:12-15; 2 Corinthians 11: 14
6. Mark 12: 25
7. 1 Corinthians 13: 12
8. Luke 21

CHAPTER 8
1. Psalm 68: 7, 9,10, 19

CHAPTER 9
1. Zechariah 9: 12

CHAPTER 10
1. Zechariah 9: 12
2. Proverbs 13:12

CHAPTER 11

1. Joel 2: 28
2. Peggy Claude-Pierre, "The Secret Language of Eating Disorders", permission granted by Abner Stein, 10 Roland Gardens, London.
3. Ibid
4. Psalm 9: 9
5. Quote and paraphrase taken from "Every Day with Jesus (Mar/Apr'81) by Selwyn Hughes; used with permission of Crusade for World Revival.
6. Psalm 139: 1,3
7. Ps.40:5
8. Isaiah 43: 1
9. 1Peter 1: 5
10. Psalm 138: 8
11. Jeremiah 31: 3
12. Isaiah 50: 4b
13. Psalm 51: 1
14. Zechariah 4: 6
15. Malachi 4: 2
16. John 14: 18
17. Psalm 34:18
18. Psalm 119: 116
19. Psalm 1: 1
20. John 7: 38
21. Proverbs 15: 1
22. Psalm 45: 2
23. John 11: 44